W9-DIU-346

EDUCATIONAL DRAMA FOR TODAY'S SCHOOLS

With an annotated bibliography

edited by

R. BAIRD SHUMAN

with chapters by

Charles R. Duke; Jan A. Guffin;
Dorothy Heathcote; R. Baird Shuman;
Betty Jane Wagner; Denny T. Wolfe, Jr.

The Scarecrow Press, Inc.
Metuchen, N.J. & London
1978

PN
3171
.E36
1978

Library of Congress Cataloging in Publication Data
Main entry under title:

Educational drama for today's schools.

Bibliography: p.
Includes index.
1. Drama in education--Addresses, essays, lectures.
I. Shuman, Robert Baird. II. Duke, Charles R.
PN3171.E36 371.33'2 78-15115
ISBN 0-8108-1166-9

Copyright © 1978 by R. Baird Shuman

Manufactured in the United States of America

4114464

In Memory of

Winifred Ward

1884-1975

CONTENTS

*This paper first appeared in Illinois Schools Journal, 56 (Winter 1976-77), pp. 3-11 and is reprinted here with the express permission of the Illinois Schools Journal and the trustees of Chicago State University.

ACKNOWLEDGMENTS

No book comes to fruition without the assistance of many people. The editor of *Educational Drama for Today's Schools* must acknowledge some specific debts. His first exposure to educational drama as an instructional medium came at a meeting of the Virginia Association of Teachers of English in Richmond some years ago when Frances N. Wimer arranged for the showing of Dorothy Heathcote's "Improvised Drama, Part I," in which a group of Scottish reform school boys improvised a drama on killing the President.

Largely on the basis of this film, the editor encouraged two of his doctoral students, Charles R. Duke and Jan A. Guffin, to pursue doctoral research in the area of creative dramatics, and each produced a strikingly strong dissertation at Duke University. Charles Duke's dissertation has since been published by the National Council of Teachers of English under the title *Creative Dramatics and English Teaching* (Urbana, Ill., 1974).

The editor first met Dorothy Heathcote in June 1975 when she came to North Carolina under the joint auspices of Wake Forest University and the North Carolina Department of Public Instruction to do teacher workshops. North Carolina's State Superintendent of Schools, A. Craig Phillips, and his able deputy, Jerome Melton, encouraged the director of the Division of Languages, Dr. Denny T. Wolfe, Jr., to bring Ms. Heathcote to North Carolina and were instrumental in finding funding for this enterprise. Other English consultants in the Division of Languages, Hathia Hayes, C. C. Lipscomb, and M. Lawrence Tucker, also worked strenuously to arrange the details of the Heathcote visit.

Largely as a result of Ms. Heathcote's North Carolina presentations, the editor proposed a three-day workshop on educational drama at the 1976 Annual Convention of the National Council of Teachers of English in Chicago. Dr.

John Maxwell of NCTE spoke on behalf of this proposal and was instrumental in obtaining approval of it. Sister Rosemary Winkeljohann, also of NCTE, handled the many details of seeing that the workshop ran smoothly, assuming responsibility for getting materials to the participants in advance of the meeting, and seeing to it that a rather intricate array of equipment was available to the workshop presenters when they needed it. Anne Thurman of Northwestern University and Betty Jane Wagner of the National College of Education in Evanston, Ill., arranged for the workshop presenters to have groups of school children to work with throughout the workshop so that the participants could see improvisations taking place.

As the papers from the workshop began to take form as a book, Dorothy Heathcote agreed to write a lead chapter and Betty Jane Wagner provided two chapters which were necessary to balance the book.

The North Carolina Department of Public Instruction was generous in making photographs available for use in the book. Ms. Florence Blakely of the Perkins Library at Duke University helped the editor when he thought he had reached an impasse in getting some illustrative material for the book.

The editor's interest in creative dramatics has been intensified by the enthusiasm of some of the teachers with whom he has dealt in various capacities. Among these many teachers, Robert C. Baird, Jr., of LeRoy Martin Junior High School in Raleigh, N.C., Leslie Hunt of the North Carolina School of the Arts in Winston-Salem, N.C., James Williams, formerly of Enloe Senior High School in Raleigh, and Gary W. Streit of Olivet Nazarene College in Kankakee, Ill., must be named specifically. The editor's students, both at Duke University and at the University of Illinois at Urbana-Champaign, have been cooperative and enthusiastic participants in many improvisations.

Finally, a deep debt of gratitude must go to three people who have helped to prepare the typescript for the publisher: Paula Cagla of Duke University, Carolyn Matthews of the North Carolina Department of Public Instruction, and Eileen Posluszny of the University of Illinois at Urbana-Champaign.

R. B. S.

INTRODUCTION

Educational drama--or creative dramatics, if one prefers that term--gained great popularity in schools during the 1920s and 1930s when the late Winifred Ward established training programs in this educational activity as part of the teacher training program at Northwestern University. Miss Ward began her teaching career at Northwestern in 1918 when she was employed to teach in the School of Speech. Some six years later she pioneered in making creative dramatics a part of the curriculum in the School of Speech. During the 32 years that she taught at Northwestern, she associated herself closely with the public schools of Evanston, which became laboratories for testing out her theories and methodologies regarding creative dramatics. Miss Ward trained many of the leaders in the educational drama movement in the United States and had a profound impact upon American education through such books as Creative Dramatics: For the Upper Grades and Junior High School (New York: D. Appleton-Century, 1930), Playmaking with Children (New York: D. Appleton-Century, 1947; 2nd ed., 1957), and Theatre for Children (Anchorage, Ky.: Children's Theatre Press, 1939; rev. ed., 1950; 3rd ed., rev., 1958).

For ten years, Northwestern laid sole claim in this country to offering work in creative dramatics. However, as Miss Ward's students began their teaching careers, her influence began, through them, to spread. In the twenty-year period from 1934 to 1954, twenty colleges and universities instituted separate courses in educational drama. In the four years between 1954 and 1958, thirty more added such offerings. A mere five years later (1963), 132 institutions of higher learning reported offering courses in creative dramatics and 277 offered courses in children's drama.[1] Although statistics are not available for more recent years, the trend has continued. Interest in educational drama received considerable impetus from the Anglo-American Conference on the Teaching of English held at Dartmouth College in 1966. Charles Duke writes, "The tremors sent out in

1966 by the Anglo-American Conference on the Teaching of English held at Dartmouth College are still being felt in many areas of the teaching of English, especially in drama. People such as James Moffett and Douglas Barnes urged that English teachers consider drama from another viewpoint besides the one of drama as merely another genre. They suggest that drama may provide a focusing element for all we normally teach in the English classroom."[2]

Emphasis on the open classroom and the awakening of interest in the functioning of the right brain, along with critiques of the formality and formalism of American education found in such landmark works as the two widely disseminated reports of the Dartmouth Conference, John Dixon's Growth through English (Reading, England: National Association for the Teaching of English, 1967) and Herbert Muller's The Uses of English (New York: Holt, Rinehart & Winston, 1967), as well as in Charles E. Silberman's Crisis in the Classroom (New York: Random House, 1970), which was aimed at a popular audience, paved the way for an increased interest in the uses of educational drama as a classroom activity and teaching device during the early 1970s. Coincident with these events was the emergence on the American scene of Dorothy Heathcote, who, for almost twenty years, had been advancing the cause of educational drama in Britain. Heathcote, a lecturer in educational drama at the University of Newcastle-upon-Tyne, visited Northwestern University in 1972, in 1974, and again in 1977, and three of her films, Improvised Drama I and ... II, outgrowths of the earlier visits to Northwestern, and Three Looms Waiting, brought her to the attention of countless American teachers. Heathcote has been a frequent visitor to this country since, giving workshops at Wake Forest University, serving as a consultant for the North Carolina Department of Public Instruction, participating in conventions of the National Council of Teachers of English, and returning periodically to various parts of the United States.

In order to understand the term educational drama as it is used in this book, it is necessary to understand what it means to Dorothy Heathcote. A developed statement of what Heathcote means by the term is found in a paper which she prepared for the Northwestern University Summer Workshop of 1974. In this paper she describes educational drama as a process which involves "playing for ourselves, in order that we may better understand the world and make acquaintance with it and the heritage and legends of it, towards learning to create within a group and finding language to communicate to each other in that group, and now towards the interpretation of other people's ideas of the world which leads us to our own understanding of the world and to our awareness of the place of the theatre or the television or the film or the novel or the poem in our world."[3]

Heathcote provided an earlier definition of the term educational drama in her paper "Drama and Education: Subject or System?" This definition is also useful and serviceable to an understanding of Heathcote's approach to the subject: "I define educational drama as being 'anything which involves persons in active-role-taking situations in which attitudes, not characters, are the chief concern, lived at life-rate (i.e. discovery at this moment, not memory based) and obeying the natural laws of the medium.'"[4] In the same essay, Heathcote stresses that more attention needs to be focused on drama as a system rather than as a subject.

Fundamental to Heathcote's definition of educational drama is her definition of drama succinctly stated in Three Looms Waiting: "Drama is not rocks and fairies and people leaping about in leotards. Drama is a real man in a mess!" If drama is a real person in a mess, then educational drama as Heathcote perceives it projects a situation that poses a dilemma and the drama unfolds as the dilemma is examined by the participants in the drama, who are working toward a resolution. In so working, they escape from themselves into another being. Just as reading literature helps one to experience vicariously events, situations, and emotions which cannot be experienced at first hand, so does educational drama enable students to get inside the consciousness of other beings and to experience a critical segment of life as those beings experience it. In that way, the enacting of an educational drama takes students a step beyond reading and plunges them into an activity in which they assume personae while at the same time creating the forward thrust of what is being enacted by composing their roles as they go along. At best they do this unselfconsciously and with considerable fluency, becoming so enrapt in their roles that they create convincing and appropriate dialogue.

Whereas Winifred Ward and many of her followers had students base their endeavors upon literature and involved them in warm-up activities prior to their enacting the drama itself, Heathcote characteristically has students invent situations and move into these situations without warm-up activities. Speaking of how Heathcote works, Robin Hall observes, "There are no preliminaries, no warm-up exercises. There is no watering down.... Working with an entire group as a unit, and sometimes taking part herself, she guides the children quickly and surely to the heart of the dramatic problem at hand. The confrontation is real."[5]

Heathcote more than anyone else has demonstrated that educational drama, as she defines it, is a process in which people at any age or level of development can engage productively. She has worked and achieved startling results with groups of boys in reformatories, with students suffering from severe learning disabilities, with girls in a home for unwed mothers, with pre-school children, elementary school children, secondary school youngsters, college students, and a large variety of teachers in in-service workshops. Many of her techniques are used also in psycho- and socio-drama and in encounter groups.

<u>Educational Drama for Today's Schools</u> begins with a lengthy, poetic essay that Dorothy Heathcote wrote specifically for this book. This essay is drastically different from anything that she has thus far produced. It is the product of a great deal of hard and penetrating thought about drama as a learning medium. She writes, "For many years I have remained unable to answer even one good reason why learning through the net of a dramatic event, whether invented or interpreted, could make it possible for some force for learning to be released. Now I have some, so please share them with me as you read." Throughout her essay, Heathcote's personal warmth and human concern are evident. Her writing makes the reader feel close to her, one with her. Although the Heathcote essay has a strong theoretical framework, it details specific, practical strategies for using drama as a system of teaching.

Heathcote emphasizes that dramatic activity of the kind she practices and is promoting enlivens students and may have long-term benefits for them: "When the capacity for reflection is awakened," she writes in this essay, "it brings about the capacity also to re-meet experiences, no matter how often they occur, and never find them dull."

The remaining chapters in the book deal with educational drama in relation to those areas of education which have received the most considerable national emphasis and attention in recent years: creativity, values clarification, language development, moral education, the basics, and hemisphericity. Each of these areas is the subject of a chapter and builds a bridge between educational drama and another major area of educational concern, showing how educational drama, as a system, can be used successfully and effectively in correlation with other modern educational strategies.

The chapter on creativity, by R. Baird Shuman, suggests ways of identifying creative youngsters within the school setting and ways of dealing with such students to foster their creativity. The chapter presents an overview of some recent research into creativity by such specialists as Paul Torrance, Ross Mooney, Taher Razik, Arthur Koestler, Elizabeth Drews, Jacob Getzels, and Philip Jackson. It goes on to give specific instructions for involving all students in dramatic activities that will enhance their self-confidence and creativity and will build sequentially from the simple to the quite complex.

Before focusing on values clarification, Charles Duke provides the reader with a framework for developing role-playing activities in the classroom. Such activities, which are a fundamental part of using educational drama as a vehicle for values clarification, are presented clearly and in sufficient detail that even the uninitiated will easily be able to follow the directions within a classroom setting. Duke ties in role playing and educational dramatics with the pioneering work in values clarification done by Merrill Harmin, Louis E. Raths, and Sidney Simon, as well as with later work by Gene Stanford and Albert E. Roark.

Fundamental to human communication is language development. Students who participate regularly in educational drama are forced to work with words and to invent linguistically. Betty Jane Wagner points out that "because participants make up the details as they go along, they not only are pressed to produce language, but they capture the vitality and tension of spontaneous human interaction as well." Wagner notes that as students move away from egocentricity through involvement in educational drama, as they learn to take on new personae, they gain in fluency and their discussion skills are thereby enhanced. They are able to carry over into other areas of the curriculum than language arts the skills which educational drama has enabled them to sharpen. Wagner stresses that educational drama is hard work and is fundamentally a school discipline unto itself. She warns, "Drama should never be viewed as just a way to sugar-coat facts; they may be learned in other and often more efficient ways." She goes on to assert that "drama is nothing less than the 'basic skill' that is the foundation of all language development."

Denny T. Wolfe's chapter, "Educational Drama and Moral Development," focuses on Lawrence Kohlberg's work in moral education, relating it lucidly with the earlier work of Jean Piaget, who provided fundamental insights into the question in The Moral Judgment of the Child (1948). Wolfe also cites the contributions of Elliot Turiel and Carol Gilligan and provides the reader with some of the results of the Invitational Conference on Moral Development which the Educational Testing Service sponsored in 1974. Wolfe suggests significant moral dilemmas with which teachers and their classes might deal dramatically in such ways that the moral development of the participants would be stimulated according to the Kohlberg taxonomy. He also classifies various literature frequently encountered in schools according to Kohlberg's stages of moral development and suggests literature that might be used as a basis for educational drama aimed at moral education of the kind with which Kohlberg concerns himself.

In an age of accountability, when the masses are demanding a return to the basics, it is necessary to be able to document the fact that educational drama is not a frill or a play activity which merely provides respite from such basic activities as spelling drill, grammar lessons, or writing exercises, but rather that it is itself a fundamental means by which students can be brought to the basics in ways that are purposeful, effective, and palatable to them. Having observed a series of demonstrations by Dorothy Heathcote in 1975, Wolfe identified 16 basic academic and behavioral skills that were either taught in the sessions or were outgrowths of them. They were newspaper reading and reporting; values clarification; intercultural exploration; vocabularly development; self-awareness and self-expression; creative and critical thinking; cooperative effort; self-discipline; perceiving implications and drawing inferences; following directions; decision making; making commitments and accepting responsibility; developing community concern; clear and effective articulation; listening; and conceptualizing.[6] To this list one can add all manner of basic instruction that can be a part of educational drama, including some very important instruction in basics which most schools have systematically overlooked in areas such as listening. Joseph Mersand addresses the dearth of instruction in listening and calls for greater emphasis on this important skill in "Why Teach Listening?," in which he writes, "Listening has been so familiar to us as a daily experience that we have taken for granted that it has been developed in our students. It is only within recent years that we have begun to realize that, just as students now come into the secondary school unable to read, so they are unable to grasp meanings, concepts, appreciations through listening."[7] But the student who participates in educational drama must learn to be an accurate listener and interpreter of what he hears, else he will be unable to participate in the drama.

In "Educational Drama and the Basics," Jan Guffin concerns himself equally with the "old" basics, the ones that laymen--as well as many professionals--are demanding a return to, and with the "new" basics, those fundaments which today's students need to develop if they are to be able to function optimally in the real world of which they are a part. Guffin suggests dramatic approaches to such matters as vocabulary and language study under the heading of "Practical Concerns," noting, "Since drama has been recognized throughout our century as the most integrated of the arts, its promise for the teacher concerned with basics is manifold." In this part of his chapter, he gives close attention to methods by which students can come to recognize and appreciate the means by which information is integrated and organized, skills that are required for anyone who would write coherently. However, Guffin's focusing upon the practical has not diverted him from broadening his consideration to include the philosophical. In the second half of his chapter, he devotes his attention to "the 'new basics' which others are suggesting American education should move forward to." The crux of his consideration comes in his statement, "No teacher is in a more auspicious position to participate in constructive change than the teacher of educational drama. One who understands the residual powers in dramatics activities for integrating personal and academic experiences, for interrelating subject areas, and for contributing to the personal and social growth of the individual cannot help viewing such change with excitement." Guffin's chapter offers a convincing rationale for including educational drama in the curricula of even the most conservative schools, those most devoted to basic education.

Betty Jane Wagner's chapter, "Educational Drama and

the Brain's Right Hemisphere," presents the fullest account yet in print of the close relationship that exists between educational drama and the development of the "right brain," the hemisphere that is all but neglected in today's schools where reason is valued over intuition, analysis over synthesis. Wagner offers the reader a splendid overview of recent work in hemisphericity done by Jerome Bruner, Robert Ornstein, Paul Bradwein, Robert Samples, and a host of others. She presents a useful contrastive table showing the difference between left- and right-brain functions and concludes her table with four insightful contrastive pairs: Observing/Meditating, Active/Receptive, Clear/Subtle, and Day/Night. Wagner warns that teachers "are going to have to face the bracing challenge of educating the public that supports the schools to the validity of right-brained understanding. This kind of learning will not lend itself to easily measurable student behavioral change; it will instead remain dark and inaccessible to left-brained accountability measuring devices." Wagner goes on to demonstrate some strategies in educational drama that she has used with groups of youngsters in the Demonstration School of the National College of Education to evoke right-brained functioning from them. She also gives detailed firsthand accounts of other demonstrations in which educational drama has succeeded in stimulating right-brained reactions from the participants.

The concluding chapter, by R. Baird Shuman, is reprinted from the Illinois Schools Journal. It deals in part with educational drama (creative dramatics) but is also concerned with the place of other dramatic activities, including play production for audiences, in schools. The author notes that drama provides opportunities for every student in the school to participate in an activity. The student who is too shy to act may contribute to school productions by handling lighting or costuming. The student who could not possibly compete in varsity athletics may act so well as to gain the sort of acclaim that the star quarterback enjoys. Schools that give more time, money, and effort to athletics than to drama may well be ignoring all but a small handful of the students it is serving, and in most cases that athletes are male so that girls are relegated to the cheerleaders' bench. This final chapter calls for a renewed emphasis on drama in schools as a means of involving a large segment of the school population in a school activity and as a means of increasing community involvement with schools.

Educational drama is currently well ensconced in

many curricula, and interest in the field is growing. A number of the chapters in this book have grown out of papers presented at a three-day workshop on creative dramatics held immediately prior to the annual meeting of the National Council of Teachers of English in Chicago on November 22-24, 1976. This pre-convention workshop was well attended by a broad range of teachers who had either been experimenting with educational drama in their own teaching situations or were eager to find out how to initiate this approach with students. Many have reported since that they are employing with considerable success some of the techniques suggested at the workshop.

A great task yet remains to be done to try to assess scientifically whether exposure to educational drama affects children's creativity. The only major study of the subject is a very limited one. It focuses on a group of 78 kindergarten students, 39 of whom were exposed to a systematic program of educational drama and 39 of whom--the control group--did not have such exposure. The experimenters were testing the hypothesis, "Classes in creative dramatics would produce significant differences in creativity" among the youngsters tested. The researchers report, "Two types of creativity measures were used for this study. One was based on visual cues and the other on verbal cues."

The results of the study suggest that students exposed to educational drama score higher on tests of creativity than those who are not exposed to it: "The two experimental groups, taken together, scored higher on the creativity tests than did the control group. The difference in the group means was significant at the .05 level of confidence. The hypothesis of the study was supported."[8]

There seems little question that activities such as those presented in this book will broaden the educational experiences of those who participate in them. Such activities will lead students to assume responsibility and become more self-reliant. They will also engage their intellectual curiosity and lead them forth in a quest for knowledge, an outcome which has everything to do with the success and failure of any educational tactic.

R. Baird Shuman

Professor of English
and Director of English Education
University of Illinois, Urbana-Champaign

References

[1]As reported by Geraldine Brain Siks in "An Appraisal of Creative Dramatics," Educational Theatre Journal 17 (December 1965), 328-29.

[2]Charles R. Duke, "Drama," in R. Baird Shuman, ed., Creative Approaches to the Teaching of English: Secondary (Itasca, Ill.: F. E. Peacock, Publishers, 1974), p. 91.

[3]Loc. cit., pp. 43-44.

[4]In Nigel Dodd and Winifred Hickson, eds., Drama and Theatre in Education (London: Heinemann, 1971), p. 43.

[5]Robin Hall, "Educational Drama in England," Children's Theatre Review 22 (January 1973), 17.

[6]From "Creative Dramatics as a Tool for Learning," North Carolina Education 6 (November 1975), 15.

[7]In Joseph Mersand, ed., The English Teacher: Basic Traditions and Successful Innovations (Port Washington, N.Y.: Kennikat Press, 1977), p. 123.

[8]Toni Schmidt, Elissa Goforth, and Kathy Drew, "Creative Dramatics and Creativity: An Experimental Study," Educational Theatre Journal 27 (March 1975), 111-14.

<u>Of These Seeds Becoming:</u>

DRAMA IN EDUCATION

Dorothy Heathcote

Someone said, "Write me some words."
I said, "Yes, if I can."
"By a certain date," said that someone.
"Yes, if I can," said I.
The date is come. I am not ready, yet must fulfil the promise made.
It has always been thus in "writing myself down" into print.

Dear reader, I shall begin and see what happens to arise between the two of us.
You who hold this book in your hand, I wonder
Do you open it with curiosity?
With greed and hunger because you feel emptied of all skill
As I sometimes do?
To jibe at other's ways of thought?
Or because you have been told you must,
Or only recommended just to try?
Is your interest in the book,
Or in the name upon the cover,
Or in those names you read within?
Because my words are lame
I ask of you that as you read
You will neither <u>judge</u> all nor <u>believe</u> all that you read of me,
But rather that you <u>inquire</u>, as a man going into a labyrinth,

[Editor's Note: Dorothy Heathcote's contribution is printed in as close to its original form as possible. In presenting the chapter to me, Ms. Heathcote wrote that the manuscript "is in this form because I'm tired of trying to take my language of metaphor (my natural tongue) & twist it up for right-handed people." The contribution clearly indicates that Ms. Heathcote's right brain and left brain were both very much at work as she labored to produce it. RBS]

Or toward death, or to a new place,
Or when returning to an old familiar one
(So that things may come *to* you as you read)
Or you stumble upon them almost by chance when turning round a corner.
I ask this because I would wish my mind and yours to meet here,
Not as opponents who might clash
or friends who greet each other's wisdom,
but rather as persons who eye one another from the place we fit;
and out of the eyeing,
we are surprised into new understanding.
I will bear your presence (the presence of your eye)
as a living vibrant scanner, restless yet benign,
in my mind as I write these words; my halting thoughts
new forged, in the crucible of my teaching yesterday
as well as those thoughts I project toward my teaching of tomorrow.
As we meet upon the pages
I will try to remember you can meet my mind only out of your experience
attitude and being.
So *please* treat my thoughts as I do--
a compound of knowing and not being certain;
like a full tree already breeding seeds
which in their turn wait for their season.
The burden of these seeds is heavy,
for as the Egyptians said before me,
"I know tomorrow for I have seen yesterday."

There are many kinds of blossoms on my teaching tree.
(And on yours?)
The many outward shapes which carry the matrixes of my work
(Those outer forms, by which the work of teachers manifests itself)
must change to suit immediate needs,
as expressions change upon faces, when in different kinds of talk
and sharing of feelings with companions.
So as I wrote to you, with you in my mind's careful eye,
I see simultaneously
blossoms of outer form so various I cannot recall them all.
For as the painter seeks to lay upon the canvas
the various, precise, passionately decorous statements
fitting for the condition of his mind's perception,
So it is with teaching.

Dorothy Heathcote (courtesy of the North Carolina Department of Public Instruction).

What classes seem to do when in my presence
rarely more than tips the iceberg
of the purposes which I and they intend.

I join myself with you, dear reader, at this moment so
that we may contemplate
some of the extraordinary, special-hewn, "one-of" models
You and I have helped create, each in our separate lives.
No two are the same, as we both know.
All differently colored, differently dynamic, differently
formed;
In space and in words upon the air;
Different in their plot and theme and style of meaning and
projection.
And we know also this most clearly--
The outer form is the product, in all art, of the mind's
meaning,

being pressed, blown, molded (in the modern sense of technical,
as well as of the ancient anthropological)
by the determined minds of myself and of my students
together with the idea's nature; and the myth memory of all of us
also shapes this form.
The journey from the nature to the form
is often quite unseen *in* the form.
Therefore it is difficult when we view the work of others
to know that (a) there *was* a struggle,
and (b) the struggle brought living to the strugglers;
that the outer form came not from some smooth stream
as often seems the case when we watch others as they work.
Often our own work seems so labored compared with what we see in theirs.
Reader, take heart--*we share the same journey*.
THE NEW GROWTH OF THE SEEDS is what we try to share with our students.

The outer form--the accomplished fact which we so often try to hurry them toward--
is *not* the learning part.
All too often the struggle--
the part which lies between the starting and the outer completing,
is seen as a necessary evil--to be got past as quickly as we may.

If I have any teaching wisdom, it is that I have learned to know
the struggle IS the learning process;
and the skills of teaching lie
in making this time slow enough for inquiry;
interesting enough for loitering along the way;
rigorous enough for being buffeted in the matrix of the ideas;
but with sufficient signposts seen for respite, planning, and regathering of energy
to fare forward on the way.
It is therefore, dear reader, my task as I see it
to arm myself well for this struggle,
so as to lead my class well into this forest of ideas,
where light, dark, soft, hard, shallow, deep elements wait
so that we carry well-guarded
the *questions* to which we have as yet no answers.
The present time will provide the time to wander and press,

not the time that we must arrive.
Arrivals are those moments of being able to demonstrate our knowing,
and the wandering is the time of learning.

So the teaching skills I need are these:

1. To delay arrivals, so that time is made for trying on, turning around, testing this way and that;
2. To preserve interest and concern so that in each new examination there is chance for more understanding to take place;
3. To press and pummel during the journey in such a way that all elements come to light, and the traveler feels the journey to be there, and
4. To illuminate the parts as they come clear, and guide to the next dark patch.

Here for you to read is an example of such a forest recently traveled through by twenty young men, all of whom had been punished for offense, by being placed upon probation in the care of officers of the law, probation officers as we call them.

The action of the work.
The outer form made manifest.

The choice of place is a casino.
The game roulette
They sit around a large table
resting on their elbows and invent
outrageous amounts of cash
to place upon the black and red.
Nothing ever moves
except their own rough, red hard hands
pushing imaginary amounts of money
forward to the center.
They share no eye contact, for they are
not yet able to make such

The intention of the work.
The matter of the action.

In the slow companionship
of no pressure to act beyond the pushing of the money forward;
all the men can slowly relax and test the atmosphere,
like rats who swiftly hide in holes and hurry out of sight.
If this security can be found for them,
they will stay "to the next place"
and I may earn the right to ask them
"What do you really do here in this casino?"
Not because I need an answer --that is not my right--

frank exchange
in the presence of a "teacher."
The only words spoken are the teacher's,
"Gentlemen, place your bets" in T.V. style
Never, in two hours
does anyone move other than their hands,
yet each man gradually declares
what brought him to this place,
and soon declares his hopes in winning
and the purpose in his life of what he wins.
These words are as rough-hewn
as the hands and faces in the room
and no moral judgment clouds the view.

but because I have the teacher's right to let them ask themselves.
After this time comes (as each bet is placed)
a tallying of their values and their ways of life
"invented" into the fabric of the "play"
and in this manifestation some small beginnings of reflection can occur,
well hidden in the action and exchange.
I hear "loneliness" and "no family" and "needs of men" come into the space.

Each nation inducts its people into a certain designated speed and pressure vortex
in which the individual must find a place to be, and a way of be-coming.
Each nation also provides some formal learning place
as a bower in a garden,
where what it values, or deems essential,
may be learned in peace.

Does it not seem strange to you, dear reader, that in the West
the "bowers" we have created
rush our clients through even faster and more pressurized than life itself imposes?
We may not stop our life nor cease the constant battery of signals,
symbolic behavior, role demands or pressure to behave in predictable ways
(that is if we wish to remain acceptable to our fellows).
Yet we have created a bower in which "learning to use this pressure fruitfully"

cannot be obtained.
Instead of a place of peace and time stretched out to give us time,
while we master ourselves, understand our natures,
gird ourselves to battle with our future (in "fine fettle" sense),
find out what our future <u>might</u> become
Forging those elements of patience to delay,
curiosity to seek out, relationships to matter, people and ideas to be explored,
we have built a place in which mostly force-feeding (as of geese) takes place.

Why is it that at some time our culture allowed teachers to assume
that all the learning a person does
will occur within this so-called bower, the school?
When did it occur that "learning a little bit" about a great deal of unconnected affairs
became respectable?
When did it occur that "turn this way, then that way, never your way"
became the pattern of the dance?
Was it when a puritanical god found the devil in little children?
Was it when we lost our contact with the making/growing processes
which unite us with all other processes of burgeoning and of dying?
Was it perhaps when we loved the proliferate things we found that we could make?
Or was it when the making of such things for profit gave men leisure
to build empires and colonies of teachers
who, freed from hewing wood and fetching water,
could produce their own varied fields and patches
with their "Keep-off" signs displayed?
If these are true, then surely the devil does give idle hands business to do.
And what a tangle we have woven round us--
for since that time we have become self-generative
of all the petty time-consuming facts and acts
we lay upon those younger than ourselves.
Sometimes, dear reader, do you ever visit the garden of your mind
and, sitting quiet there, do you ever dream of the grace that might come
into this bower, the school, if people might be permitted

to become obsessed by just a few important matters?
Where one thing might lead naturally to another?
Where inquiry might have time?
Where discipline is from a subject rather than another person?
Where people might "learn themselves" into the work?
Where small persons and big persons might grow together
and help each other learn?
Where teachers and students might garden and grow
and dig and delve and argue and tell and ask,
and develop on each other, rather than submitting and arguing about submission?
The more I teach the more I start to understand
that the essential elements I need, in the work I wish to foster,
are times of incubation and reflection on their actions
and talking out their notions into their understanding,
even though within the seeming "mad house" we have made the enterprise
(dreamed up with so much honor in the conception) our schools.
All this, of course, dear reader, will smack of self-indulgence,
if you have not listened carefully to the elements of rigor
self-discipline and pressure the artist lays upon himself
because the work he does must of necessity begin to rule him;
Within those straits of fighting for the only certain form
to bring into fruition the ideas he struggles to make clear.
Why is it that we have steadfastly refused,
except in certain places which give harbor, for real teaching to take place,
(and such persons and such places seem to spring
almost at random like poppies in a field of English corn)
to allow our schools to work on tasks large enough
to make the doing worth the doing?

For many years I have remained unable
to answer even one good reason why
learning through the net of a dramatic event,
whether invented or interpreted,
could make it possible for some force for learning to be released.
Now I have some, so please share them with me as you read.
Are they not the most common of common-sense?

1. Thinking from within a situation forces a different type of thinking;
2. Sharing thinking, bouncing it off other's thought, keeps thought fluidly in action;

yet it constantly clears away fog, so that I begin to know
the content and the context of my thought
which moves me forward to my next endeavor
somewhat informed of why.

3. Keeping in touch with universal myths and themes
(the means which men have found
to explain themselves and their place in the world's pattern and design)
keeps me in touch with myself to recognize the forces in myself
at deeper levels than the task-level living of my life.
Where are the places a child may enter to learn that there are no
"only task" levels in a life which truly will be lived?
Who provides place and guide in this matter
if the place we have named the school ignores the seeking out?

4. Building a language for expression
and a language for reflection
is important in the growth of people
so that they remain in touch with who and what they themselves are.

5. Trying on all types of experiences in safety,
from those of science to fighting mighty evil
or striving to perform great good,
is important in my "forming of myself" to accept
and live fruitfully in the twin world of technology and humanity--as I must.
These five are in some part fostered through dramatic experience
though others share the field with equal honor.

These questions were asked by children recently, of themselves, while working in dramatic mode,
Sometimes in verbal, sometimes in action "talk,"
Some directly to me, many of themselves, not involving me directly.
"Does the sap of plants work as the blood of humans?"
"Do people ever miss their parents (when grown up), if they die, as children do?"
"How can one know when making a promise, one can ever keep it?"
"Why do we seek promises of those we love?"

"Why does one country feel it must help another?"
"Are nations formed by the land they live in?" "How does forming then occur?"
"Will the sun ever fail to rise?"
"Is there an Apollo? Was there ever one? Would it feel safer if there were?"
For these questions to ever see the light of day
we must keep silence, within structured possibility till they form.
Neither must we think that abdication from the pressure
to lead into the areas where they may occur, is a proper teaching place to be.

So the outer blossoms of my tree are variously shaped
and the many delayed arrivals are each unique and different journeys
feeding me, not emptying me. I do not give out to others; They do not receive from me my knowing;
I live with and on their ideas, they live on and with mine.
I have a gift of inheritance from each class I teach,
as well as from those who gave me life.
Are we not the same, dear reader?
Is it not here we truly meet
as we eye each other across the space of different ways and places?
Greetings in the new joining of our inheritance from our classes.

Here is a corner we might turn together.
I see us in a labyrinth where roads bend and twist.
This road I shall call "The road of experience and reflection upon experience."
These things I have come to realize--
that all my teaching life, whether planning to teach,
or teaching, I have sought to marry closely two things in closest fashion.
The catharsis and anagnorisis of the Greek's naming:
The experience possible in any learning journey
and the reflection upon that experience at the very moment
or as close to it as possible.
All my teaching lures, strategies and skills seek this marriage.
It is my golden key to my mind's working and my practice.
For I believe experience without reflection
leaves the person hungering for more.
The act without digestion never feeds the growth.
Rather it destroys the savor, and the act then

becomes in-experience, boredom, repetition--
always seeking a new flavor--a new seeming change.
Reflection creates new acts, not copies of the old, though they may be the same acts,
in their outer form, and brings new flavor, constantly, to the doing.
So every teaching tool I have
has been hewn to supply and feed reflection.
These are some I understand and have brought from my left hand
of intuition to my right hand of reason and therefore of conscious application, to my work.

(1) In each situation I have the instinct to play a role at first
WITHIN THE DRAMA. This is often seen by doubters as my entering the play
so as to take away the matter from my classes
or to interfere with their ideas.
I enter a role into the situation so that
without interrupting the flow of their action or of thought,
I can instigate reflection upon the action.
It allows me to encourage their involvement and belief
because my own is present, in the situation not outside.

Example:

As the German officer, seeking to "help" a group of young delinquent boys
who have chosen to be taken prisoner, "gain" their captivity with honor
and no loss of face, in order to examine with them the matter of their lives--
the implications of being taken prisoner--for that is what they really are.
"Rouse, rouse, give up your rifles!"
at which demand they are prone to argue.
In my role I can promote this argument
but more important still than that, I can inject a reflective note
immediately without changing tempo or pace
or asking them "to think about it"--the strategy so often employed--
by saying, "I shall remember you," in a certain warning way.
This warns the group of that which will/can come about
because of their behavior up to now. The choice however will be theirs to make.

The choice catches them short. They see it, though they need not understand
all the ramifications of that choice as yet.
It changes the direction of their thought and their responses know another lilt,
so hopefully a deeper understanding of being a prisoner can occur.
They say that "lifers"--prisoners in Sing Sing--
read plays of murderers for twenty years before finding Waiting for Godot
had anything to say to them! Perhaps my tone can shift a gear a little sooner?
Suddenly the cost to themselves if they continue to argue,
becomes an issue, new within the context of the game.
And they know they have the choice to make themselves
on whether they decide to heed the suggestion or not.
Which they will choose depends on the alternatives they are at present
capable of perceiving, but the choice is NOW and seen to be THERE.

(2) I never make dramas in simulation mode,
Where that which takes place pretends to be "as it might have been."
The outer form may often show it as being so--the inner action denies this outer form.
To work in episodic fashion allows the next episode to cause reflection on the last one.

Example 1:

Pit boys-to-be after their time in school, choose the pit for their investigation.
They ask for "a disaster."
Chairs are piled in readiness for their fall of rock--and the chance to make a noise?
(And what of the mysterious pre-living of the real danger of the mine
awaiting them in years to come? Is this also present in the room?)
We then sit down beside these chairs
and talk the cracks into the rock
by speaking to the rock to bring it into action.
Do you see, dear reader,
how the talking of the rock into the action of the fall of rock
IS the reflection on the disaster, in some part?
Later, when the rock chairs are fallen on their bodies,

and these lie under and around the chairs, and all is still,
with the noise made by their mouths abated,
these same "bodies" speak of what they will remember of the moment of the disaster,
and what they believe will be the future of the mine.
Here again, reader, you will recognize the reflection built into the work,
not following after--though this also may occur, but in a different vein.

Example 2 (reflection during experience):

A group of black high school age adolescents
living in central Birmingham in England, chose to examine,
"What it would be like to be mentally handicapped."
Their interest is aroused because shortly to their school will come a unit of such people.
The simulation of being handicapped must never make us think we fully understand,
though I applaud their interest and concern to be prepared for when the time will come,
when they will meet such people (and themselves therefore anew?)
in their school.
I suggest we become lifelike dolls, made by "city fathers,"
to show the public what such a state of being really brings, to those born thus,
and to the families which must care for them.
We set ourselves the task of explaining to the public (other classes)
what being mentally handicapped brings into the home--
the constant watching over, being ready, the never-being-redundant
of the parent, sister, brother, friend.
It is the teaching demonstrations of a lifelike DOLL
which brings about reflection.
Plus the questioning from "believing" friends as to such matters
of sleeping, feeding, learning, washing of these afflicted persons.
No-one believed these dolls were real.
No-one believed they fully understood. (How could one know the half of it?)
Everyone entered for a space the "rooms" of mystery inhabited by such.
To pretend one was, could be a lessening and a travesty of the lives they have to lead.

But to give consideration in this seeming strangely life*like* way
made a platform for reflection upon such lives and matters.
In the answering of the questions they and I could hear,
the new awareness of the cost some people pay to have been born.
But not you and I, dear reader--nor those beautiful young people there in Birmingham.

I call this "protection into emotion," and in public I have been much blamed for it.
There are many faces to such protection.
You will have some--not necessarily such as mine.
I do not ask you to agree--only to recognize the need--
and supply it. And give space to mine if you do not happen to approve.
I give you space for yours. Perhaps both can exist together?
And the ambiguity of difference hold? I hope so.
I regard this capacity to protect into emotion, not avoidance of it--
to be high-priority teaching skill.
Especially when drama is the chosen mode for learning,
as in the instances I give.
For in drama there is no outside medium
to carry the idea's moulding.
The person conceiving of the idea *is* the medium by which it is expressed.
Therefore, there is in my view important need of the reflection
to become active within the experience,
so as to provide protection from too deep involvement
and to lead toward new growth.
But in order for the watcher to give it recognition,
close watch upon the inner thinking as expressed by outer handling,
must be made. The protection comes in many guises,
not always yielding up the meaning at first glance.
"New growth" to me when teaching
means that I can perceive that a shift
either of recognition or of understanding
is in process of being made.
This process must be perceivable as being demonstrated
before I will accept that it has begun.

Dear reader, do we as yet share any thoughts in common?
Do my examples make you fear?
There is no enemy awaiting you from my examples

unless placed in the pathway there by you.
Let me tell you the last and perhaps most important reason
why for me the reflection must come within the time of the experience,
or as close upon it as it may.
When *anagnorisis* can take place
within the process of *catharsis*,
those forces of arrival, and doubt,
and facts of knowing
CANNOT MASS to prevent the power of the intuition
becoming available in the process, to stand beside the reasoned reasons.
Never has intuition denied the value of the mind--except in fools--
but those processes of doubt, inbred and ever-waiting,
fear the forces of intuition.
So as a teacher I endeavor
to make the most of those moments--very rarely wakened--
when experience is an ascendency, and language freed for power to express,
so that while forces of doubt lie sleeping,
reflection upon experience, based on intuition, can spring to action.
This allows us to experience awe--the magic in the mundane,
the elegant classic exposition of the ordinary,
the phoenix rising from the dust of the familiar--and neglected--
and to know at that moment and in this time
that this is what we make of it and comprehend about it.
Such work knows no barriers of subject--
only *treatment* delicately placed into the action,
to protect the individual from any personal arising,
of fear or gorge, but neither shabbily treat the matter
into *pretense* of examination, which often passes for protection in the drama mode.
When the capacity for reflection is awakened
it brings about the capacity also to re-meet experiences,
no matter how often they occur,
and never find them dull. For we find them always newly.
The Japanese have a way of speaking of religion ...
which occupies my mind.
"For a thing to be religious, it need only be simple and repetitive."
This is how *anagnorisis* perpetually renews *catharsis*.
So as a teacher I do not fear that I shall ever not know enough
to feed my students.

There are times when I am short of facts,
(for I have learned only a little of all those that are available to be known)
but there are no times in the day
when my reflective knowing does not, cannot come to my aid.
I would wish the same to them. And to you, dear reader.
So for me to sharpen the perception and the reflective process
is more important than to store the information
I can find when needed, in other places than myself.
Not that I despise facts.
I am fascinated by the myriads of <u>things</u> which await the curious mind;
but no amount of this re-coverable information
will stand instead of knowing and perceiving from within myself.
The computers man has learned to build
will become the ever-more efficient banker for that knowing
which remains clear, precise and proven. Silver-clearly recognizable in the mists
for which there is yet no computer to dispel.
For no computer yet exists which can ingest, carry, process and exhume
the deep patterns of one's own inheritance,
or hold in factual form those gleanings from the ancient myths,
which have no shape except where abstractions large as death and heroes
have been given shape in archetypal tales,
to be summoned to stir and activate the modern mind,
and remade in shapes more fitting to that time which is not yet come.
But never to be ignored.
(For how can you ignore those major abstract forces, with no faces
except those each new generation finds to give them temporary form?)

The school, dear reader, seems to me to be,
a perfectly conceived place wherein the person, the individual we value,
can step, with full permission of the culture, for a time,
outside the world's vortex, to enable
exploration of those elements which can help to inform humanity
of new explorations to be made,
with the "passionate decorum" (J. S. Bruner) of reflective persons

who are unafraid to make such experiences in real ways
and to make the fruits of such experience a force in the world.
SUCH HUMANITY WOULD BE IRRESISTIBLE.
The world would increase itself on such.
Don't you wish, dear reader, you could be alive in such a time?
But we can now, I believe, even when such force is stacked against us,
within our lives, begin the process
by which this might come about.
For we can say (because of the endowment given us by society,
to prepare their young "to enter into their kingdom," the world of the adult),
"Here and now, the next time I teach,
whatever experiences I seek to bring about,
will have reflection built into the experience.
No longer shall experience only be enough."
We know that in our lives, at times of new illumination,
the use of the experience can only be employed
because <u>we are aware that this is now in our comprehended understanding</u>.
It is this we carry forward--not the experience itself.
Knowing that we now know it, is our computer to our future using.
Thus the true force of reason after intuition shares the power of the event.

Because this last path has wandered much,
and my words are somewhat indistinct to guide you,
shall we re-examine the corners we have turned in each other's company--
that is if you still walk beside me.
The labels I have used may not be yours,
but they are easily changed for those which suit you best.

I lay it before you as a kind of creed, but it is the map of my choosing.

1. The interior journey made in drama contains all the possible arrivals.
The interior journey is that which makes all arrivals possible.
Without the interior journey no journey will be made,
for only time will be made to pass to fill the hour.
The interior journey makes the next journey possible,

and to some extent foreshadows what it will be like.
2. The school can become a bower created for knowing how to learn
and also to recover the learning left by others for us
so that we may have such keys as their lives made possible--
and that we may protect that learning to those who follow us.
3. That certain modes of learning,
which have been denied so far,
are worthy of affirmation and respect,
the intuition serving the proven in the quest for understanding.
4. That experience and reflection
as preparation for the life outside the school
should work together to avoid the fashionable forces of doubt and indifference,
(far more damaging to culture than the fear)
overtaking intuition as a force, too, in our lives.
5. That recognition of the importance of the balance of reason and intuition
be given credence--
and that a language be forged so that both these aid the growth of individuals,
and thus enter the future cultures of the world.

Now follows an account as truly as I can recall it
of work with smallish children, aged eight to ten,
meeting daily for one hour over a period of four weeks.
I ask you, dear reader, to approach this account
in a spirit of inquiry, not comparison.
Afterwards you can then coolly place it side by side with your own inclinations.
Do not make the mistake, as some will do,
of trying to fit it to a label you would wish to give it,
and make assumption that the name you name it will be my name.
I have no labels for my work.
Neither do I have a framework other than the task I see
of that time and that place and in that context;
but I do relate this account to the matters I have discussed above.
These are the matters of my living creed,
therefore let it not be placed in any affiliation which it cannot fit.
All our work springs from what we are (as this writing does)
And how you read it springs from you.

Photos courtesy of North Carolina Department of Public Instruction.

There are no worthy names (other than loose terms)
with which we can bind one person to another by what they do.
My work has been affiliated to creative drama in the mind of some,
and then attacked because it does not fit the mold they gave it.
Our work need fit no mold given to it by others.
If it makes a change in people of some worthy kind--
and not all our work can be perfectly judged to bring about this change--
then we can call it work and leave the labeling on one side.
The work of all teachers is unique,
unless they cannot think their ideas out for themselves.
So, dear reader, I give myself no titles or big names for what I do.
Do not place an inherited weight upon it it does not deserve.
For me it is a monument of all the classes laboring to bring ideas
into some kind of knowing form, from which they might take a view,
a moment's snapshot of a newly seen idea.
I stand by my ideas because the classes I have taught
have taught me that I can trust them.
But always the black dog stalks beside, waiting to stop me in my tracks--
all teachers know this dog;
He pants beside one at every time of day,
telling one there is too much to know and not enough of knowing;
that one's ways are "wrong," "shabby," not praiseworthy--
The only thing that shakes him temporarily off one's back
is knowing the perpetual innocence (not naivete) of the new starting,
the perennial trying to live cleanly in the work of forging a personal faith,
that what one does, in thanks for being free of the hewing of wood
and the drawing of water, is done for the life to come of those given into our care.
There is space for many such in the bower which one day we may earn the right to call the school.

The year is 1975. Summer time.
Winston-Salem in North Carolina is the place.
"Bicentennial" is the chosen theme--the children's choice--
though many teachers would have wished "Old Salem" had been named.

The children made a list of those matters dear to them.
"The Declaration made in Mechlenburg";
"The Declaration of Independence";
"The freeing of slaves by Mr. Lincoln";
"The Flight of the Wright Brothers";
"Watergate";
and "Telling Mr. Ford there should be a Museum for the history which keeps coming up."
In each of these accounts that you can read,
I sought to bring into action what I believe to be important for learning through drama to take place.
I do not here list all I believe--only the ones important to the work reported here.
All I do believe in was present all the time I taught,
as presumably it is when you are teaching, dear reader.

1. Slowing matters down (though not necessarily seeming so to children)--
sometimes slow seems fast, within the context and the strategy.
I slow so that some "stumbling upon authenticity" be achieved.
2. Removing the situation when I could from prejudicial view,
so as to enable a new view without the burden of an old label
which prevents re-view.
3. Creating the experience and reflection side by side.
4. Working within the framework of that which is dramatic,
structuring so that thought and action arise
and follow through thinking and acting from within,
the trap of tension and some unities, though not always like the Greek,
of time and place and circumstance.

Most learning in the school is undertaken from without a circumstance
so thought <u>about</u> it takes place, but not thought from within.
This means, of course, the right hand of reason usually holds sway.

There is a story in the events invented by the children
to carry the passage of the history times--
A time machine of the children's designing
with help from magazines of USA technology
and a letter to NASA--we never received a reply.
Perhaps it lies on some bewildered official's desk yet?
"Can it be a letter from a spy?"

Throughout the work, no matter what the time,
the children remained always themselves in part.
It is the watcher in supportive role
who must be kept awake, so that when the child enters
the other logic of the art, the mind stays, clearly seeing
the reflector part.
I write here of the watcher we all have within--
the watcher without which the artist cannot work.
I do not mean those others present who observe the work.

This meant the class must enter that time,
into the affairs of that time,
but also in some measure, as if they
saw into each time.
This is important to remember as you read
for all the structures I created were evolved for this.
I am prepared to be instant playwright
for the threading of the class ideas as they emerge.
It is easy to miss in this, that my listening ear
and restless tongue, take trouble to inquire what matter
the class will be concerned with,
and what manner gives reflection of their depth
of interest (intuitive and academic).
The playwright sees to it that shapes are made
to carry constant shift of gear--their gears.
But often this delicate matter of the listening ear
is missed by onlookers. They only see arrivals,
not the processes of the dance.

The "removals" from the situation (where prejudice
might cloud the view,
or feeling, "that we do not know enough to try"
might make the children feel insecure)
were sometimes created by the use of roles outside the class.
The children therefore met at different times
persons from that age, whose business and affairs
we aided if we could. Always at such times
the children were in charge of the events
helping the people understand their dilemma
and show them a way through, in ways they could perceive.

1. At Mechlenburg some bewildered ladies,
shelling peas and beans outside the court house,
listened with bewilderment to the clerk
who read the statement to them.
"Not billet the King's men? How dare we not?"
It is no light thing to tell a housewife

of her rights--especially when you are only ten years old
and from another time. I overheard one child:
"I'll try to help, but I don't understand too well
about loyalty yet myself." Can one ask more?

2. In the time of the "other" independence,
Mr. Jefferson was much pressed to get his syntax right.
The hour was late, and he much tired from working on
his text.
Nothing makes you read with so much care
than when another asks you to correct their views
and spellings.
"All men are created equal" did not seem right
until they realized "treated equal" is the current curse
not "created equal." Then they let it pass.

3. In the matter of Mr. Lincoln and the slaves
they administered a Roman villa in the time of Virgil,
using his <u>Georgics</u> to help them with the planting
and harvesting of vines. They read the text of Virgil
(printed large at first, and fragmented just a little,
but never changed from the version of the translator)
when they needed recipe or guide, as if a Latin text
were an everyday matter to them--as of course it is.
The work of poets, as of engineers, is worthy of everyday use.
I don't think Virgil would find it less than healthy.
The Roman villa had to be because an English woman
has no right to create the situation where black children
and white children in a class, would fulfil by natural
self-selection
the older pattern of their nation's history.
There was evidence in their choosing of Mr. Lincoln that
some children
wished for this. An American teacher might have the
right to tackle this,
but not a visitor and guest. So the Roman villa came
to be.
The hard facts of slavery for ten-year-olds
lay not only in the work, but in the food they had to eat.
Chicken for the masters, bread for slaves.
When Mr. Lincoln arrived (at the villa, of course)
There was anachronism of place, but not of event,
or of tension, or of condition--only the minor difference
of a date and villa.
The central factor in my mind is always
that anachronism of <u>condition</u> must never be present in
the work.

All others do not matter quite so much.
It is comparatively simple to correct the facts,
but difficult always to realign the meaning.
When Mr. Lincoln came, therefore, the children asked,
as others did before them in an earlier time,
and place, "Where is there to go to, Mr. Lincoln?
We cannot return to Greece. We have no homes there.
What shall we therefore do? Can we not stay?"
Is not this the authenticity of modern Palestine?
Or the Deep South of an older time? The time they wished to see
when they chose their time machine?
This is the authenticity which drama all through time
has sought to bring into the lives of people.
"What would it have been like if I had been there?"

4. In the matter of Watergate I sensed much prejudice--
"stupid man," "cheat and liar" were their phrases.
As an English woman I yet again did not wish to structure
the circumstances in which their critical faculties worked only in a destructive mode.
Critical thought of true kind--where balance can prevail--
is hard when strong prejudice is present
and strong feelings are aroused.
To create the one remove, and reflective element in the action,
I suggested a wax museum to inform all future American children
of the facts and evidence of the time.
And somewhat of the emotions abroad just then.
Watergate is complex at the best of times.
Sorting and arranging of figures--the watching teachers--
allowed time for seeing that under each event lies much torment.
The rational ordering of the pattern of events
led to some consideration of the feeling of each event.
I remember Mr. Ford, waiting in the wings to be called
to lead the nation. At first he stood wooden, waiting to be alive.
Soon, as they saw the lack of life, they placed him in a crowd,
his life temporarily held in wait--nothing to be done--
until the proper time of answering the call to lead.
How does a man pass such a time?
They chose to make him write and rethink his speech
and throw each trivial run upon the floor around his secretary's feet,

to fill the time. To bite his nails at slow time's passing,
and telephone his family.
The slowness of arranging wax figures allowed the reflective process
to begin, and re-thinking based on the artist's views
as they surveyed their work to take over from the first thoughts.
Let us not suppose the prejudice to be gone.
That is not my business.
It seems to me my business to open, by any means I can,
another door, alongside their own opinion (or that of parental telling)
that might be worth a view.
"But this is not the matter for the teacher," you may respond--
as is your right, I have, however, given it some thought
and hold to my view of the responsibility of the teacher.

5. The Wright brothers needed other doors than prejudice.
When Concorde or a 747 is your model for a plane,
How can you see those pieces of canvas and elastic constructed
to give men a bird's eye view? They had some slight trouble with it.
until we danced and sang it into our own bodies.
Then the smallness of the container
for the mighty deeds of courage came to clearness.
I gave the form, they gave the words.
The dance we made together, and the words came as we began to understand. [See Appendix II for the poem.]

Now follow statements, dear reader, which I hope can show you
the interior thinking of my mind when conceiving of the work,
trying to read the minds of children,
considering history of a country other than my own,
and trying to shape experience meaningful to them as well as to me,
in drama mode. I give it into your hands freely
as they gave it to me. Use it if you will
in any way you find agreeable.
This is the privilege of the one who writes,
and the one who reads the writing.

MECHLENBURG DECLARATION OF INDEPENDENCE

Removal from prejudice.	Not necessary. No strong feelings except pride in their country.
Keeping awake the watcher in children. The critical element.	Having to listen to the ladies, while they listened to the declaration being read to them. Having to explain to them, what change it might bring into their lives. Having to help them to understand the actual meaning in words and to understand about England.
Dramatic form chosen so that they learn inside the event and from their particular involvement, in the event.	The ladies were shelling peas and preparing food, so it was necessary, in order not to interrupt (who interrupts their mother when food is being prepared for the family?) that they sat beside them, knowing we were not in their century, try to attract their attention, and to help if we could as we saw their distress. Mixing of times was conventionalized so there was no problem here for them.
Slowing-down device.	The reader is reading slowly, for he is not adept at it. The ladies are slow to understand and feel "not clever" at such matters. Watching from the time machine to see if we (a) want to help, and (b) if we think we can.
Inbuilt reflection.	Choosing the next time to go to can only be done by considering what other things we would wish to know about "if only we had been there." There was throughout, no simulation of an historical event. We were there, so it was different--it could not have been the same when it really happened without us.

DECLARATION OF INDEPENDENCE

Removal from prejudice.	No problem. They are delighted (with a British teacher) to explain what a good thing it was to be free of the rule of Britain.

Keeping awake the watcher in children. The critical element.	Correcting Mr. Jefferson's syntax and trying to check that he has said what he meant to say and has not forgotten anything important.
Dramatic form chosen so that they learn inside the event and from their particular involvement, in the event.	Entering his study where the candle burns low, seeing him so tired, moving to a table where a Salem lantern burns, finding quill pens there with tricorn hats and bonnets on their chairs, so they wore them. Seeing over the table to each other, only faces "in period," as it were. Pressure of time as candle burns out.
Slowing-down device.	It is a long but fascinating document--worthy of our steel--it has been typed in very large type, double spaced, so we have ample space for our corrections.
Inbuilt reflection.	When you are ten years old, correcting a large tall man's work, who seems as if he would know a lot, is a very powerful responsibility. After all, the government of America will depend somewhat on this document being right.

FREEING OF THE SLAVES

Removal from prejudice.	Much prejudice, mixed class. *They are not prejudiced against each other.* They are prejudiced each to fill the roles they would have filled in time past. This is particularly true of the black children. *I am not American.* An American teacher would have a different point of view, and would have been more able to feel out the best way than I was.
Keeping awake the watcher in children. The critical element.	Slaves kept notes on masters; masters, notes on slaves. Each was in contact all the time. One wore a cardboard lock around neck, other wore a key.
Dramatic form chosen so that	Administering a vineyard in the time of Virgil.

they learn inside the event and from their particular involvement.	Using *The Georgics* in the "office."
Slowing-down device.	Using *The Georgics* to find out what to do, and planning the work together--master and slave. One showing the other--sometimes master led, and sometimes slave, according to how each couple wanted to work. Each couple tried to help each other to lead and follow.
Inbuilt reflection.	When the owner needed explanation, they made reports. [See Appendix I.] Explaining to Mr. Lincoln what it was like being a slave, while the masters listened and in their turn reported what it is like to have to be in charge. Hearing that they were free. Writing their memoirs.

THE WRIGHT BROTHERS

Removal from prejudice.	Concorde and 747's cloud the view of how the skill of the flyer would be different.
Keeping awake the watcher in children. The critical element.	Making the plane and the flyers with bodies as well as mouths. Making the forms and shapes together with the word's meaning coming alive. The slow development of the description from body of plane to hearts of men.
Dramatic form chosen so that they learn inside the event and from their particular involvement, in the event.	The dance/poem form.
Slowing-down device.	The repetition, giving more pleasure in repeating the parts they liked, and the

Photos courtesy of the North Carolina Department of Public Instruction.

slow build-up to the "hearts of men"--by now their own hearts.

Inbuilt reflection.	Creating the words as they developed the ideas. But having much help with the words. Trying it fast and slow. Devising the patterns of movement. [See Appendix II.]

WATERGATE

Removal from prejudice.	Very necessary to get them to realize there is strong opinion now abroad--they would have heard it every day--there was no way I could think of "removing" it to another time, as with the slaves--it would have been ridiculous to contemplate.
Keeping awake the watcher in children. The critical element.	Having to make wax works get into position and plan the incident at each stage of the Watergate inquiry.
Dramatic form chosen so that they learn inside the event and from their particular involvement, in the event.	Actually making a wax museum from the very inception of the idea.
Slowing-down device.	Wax works are hard to arrange. Each arm and leg and chair and property must be selectively placed. They stand as you place them so you can look for a long time to "see if you like it like that."
Inbuilt reflection.	Writing the statement which goes beside each scene. Providing lectures to explain each scene to the public. Writing for future persons who will only have heard of Watergate from a time gone by.

MODERN HISTORY MUSEUM

Removal from prejudice.	No prejudice. Dealt directly with problems.
Keeping awake the watcher in children. The critical element.	Having to be architects actually advising the President, designing the whole thing. Locating it.
Dramatic form chosen so that they learn inside the event and from their particular involvement, in the event.	Dealing with public opinion, public funding, being responsible for all choices of spaces, developing plans, finding important exhibits.
Slowing-down device.	It is a huge complex task to do anyway. When it is for a country as large as America, all this is exacerbated to a vast complexity.
Inbuilt reflection.	Writing to President Ford our choices of venue and the report of "What a museum should seek to do for the people." [See Appendix III.] Finally, a letter from Keats to his friend Reynolds (no. 62 in the Hyder Rollins Edition).

Memory should not be called knowledge. Now it appears to me that almost any Man may, like the Spider, spin from his own inwards his own airy Citadel--the points of leaves and twigs on which the spider begins her work are few, and she fills the air with a beautiful circuiting; man should be content with as few points to tip with the fine web of his Soul, and weave a tapestry empyrean, full of symbols for his spiritual eye, of softness for his spiritual touch, of space for his wondering, of distinctness for his LUXURY. It has been an old comparison for our urging on--the Bee Hive--however it seems to me that we should rather be the Flower than the Bee; let us not, therefore, go hurrying about and collecting honey-bee like, buzzing here and there impatiently from a knowledge of what is to be arrived at; but let us open our leaves like a flower and be passive and reflective.

It does not say all truth, dear reader, for me;

I value the active as well as the passive, receptive parts of me;
Nevertheless there is some truth in Keats' letter for me
When I consider teaching and the art of creating learning circumstances
For others. May you fare well in your classrooms.

Appendix I "Freeing of the Slaves" (reports made after discussion with children)

What is a slave? Someone who:

1. May not go anywhere without consent or without directives
2. Must live under the shadow of arbitrary decisions grown out of the wishes, whims of others.
3. Must find his value mostly from within himself.
4. Must be subject to the weighing of Money Price
5. Seeks to find a life balance out of his skill in reading the minds/wishes/attitudes of others
6. Masks his signals--with careful discretion
7. Anticipates a variety of Rewards/Punishments

What is a slave owner? Someone who:

Must at all times carry the burden of decision
Must at all times be prepared to
justify-act-explain
tolerate-direct-resolve
Uses labor productively
Knows himself as master--whatever that may mean to him
Preserves with each individual the due space:
1. Territoriality
2. Status
Teaches-Learns simultaneously
Selects & Chooses & Apportions
Men/Money/Aspiration

Appendix II The Song/Dance on "The Wright Brothers" (modeled on "The house that Jack built")

This is the plane the Wright Brothers built;

These are the nuts that fasten the plane
that the Wright Brothers built;

These are the bolts that joined the nuts that
fasten the plane
that the Wright Brothers built;

This is the wood that holds the bolts
that join the nuts
that fasten the plane that the Wright Brothers built;

This is the cross of body and wing,
made of the wood
that hold the bolts
that join the nuts
that fasten the plane that the Wright Brothers built;

These are the struts that glue the wings,
that join the cross
made of the wood
that holds the bolts
that join the nuts,
that fasten the plane that the Wright Brothers built;

This is the cloth that covers the form
over the struts,
that glue the wings,
that join the cross
made of the wood
that holds the bolts
that join the nuts
that fasten the plane that the Wright Brothers built;

This is the stick that steers the plane,
inside the cloth that covers the form,
over the struts,
that glue the wings
that join the cross
made of the wood
that holds the bolts
that join the nuts
that fasten the plane that the Wright Brothers built;

This is the wire that fixes the tail
joined to the stick,
that steers the plane,
inside the cloth that covers the form,

over the struts,
that glue the wings,
that join the cross,
made of the wood,
that holds the bolts,
that join the nuts,
that fasten the plane that the Wright Brothers built;

This is the tail that turns on the wire
that fixes the tail
joined to the stick,
that steers the plane
inside the cloth that covers the form,
over the struts,
that glue the wings,
that join the cross,
made of the wood,
that holds the bolts,
that join the nuts
that fasten the plane that the Wright Brothers built;

This is the power that goes to the tail,
that turns on the wire
that fixes the tail
joined to the stick
that steers the plane,
inside the cloth that covers the form
over the struts,
that glue the wings,
that join the cross,
made of the wood,
that holds the bolts,
that join the nuts,
that fasten the plane that the Wright Brothers built;

These are the men that built in the power
that goes to the tail,
that turns on the wire
that fixes the tail
joined to the stick
that steers the plane,
inside the cloth that covers the form
over the struts,
that glue the wings,
that join the cross,
made of the wood,
that holds the bolts,

that join the nuts
that fasten the plane that the Wright Brothers built;

These are the hearts that beat in the men
that built in the power
that goes to the tail
that turns on the wire
that fixes the tail
joined to the stick
that steers the plane,
inside the cloth that covers the form
over the struts,
that glue the wings,
that join the cross,
made of the wood,
that holds the bolts,
that join the nuts,
that fasten the plane that the Wright Brothers built;

This is the hope which beats in the hearts
that beat in the men
that built in the power
that goes to the tail
that turns on the wire
that fixes the tail
joined to the stick
that steers the plane,
inside the cloth that covers the form
over the struts,
that glue the wings,
that join the cross,
made of the wood,
that holds the bolts,
that join the nuts,
that fasten the plane that the Wright Brothers built;

We are the folks who watch the hope
which beats in the hearts
that beat in the men
that built in the power
that goes to the tail
that turns on the wire
that fixes the tail
joined to the stick,
that steers the plane
inside the cloth that covers the form,
over the struts,

that glue the wings,
that join the cross,
made of the wood,
that holds the bolts,
that join the nuts
that fasten the plane that the Wright Brothers built.

Appendix III Letters/Enclosures

WAKE FOREST UNIVERSITY
Winston-Salem, North Carolina

July 12th 1975.

Dear Mr President,

I enclose a typed note and signatures of the delightful class I have taught this year in Winston-Salem. They did not really expect that they could write to their busy President and receive a reply but as an English woman I felt that they would! So I decided to send the letter to you and I shall see that the class have your reply when it arrives. I seem to have more faith than they do. Please forgive having to give time in a busy schedule to our request, but it is in a good cause. The class are 10 and 11 year olds.

Yours sincerely,

(Mrs.) Dorothy Heathcote

Senior Lecturer,
School of Education,
University of Newcastle-upon-Tyne,
St Thomas' Street,
Newcastle on Tyne,
England. NEI 7RU.

*****

WAKE FOREST UNIVERSITY
Winston-Salem, North Carolina 27109

Department of Speech Communication
and Theatre Arts
Box 7347

July 12, 1975

Dear Mr. President,

We are a class of children working with a teacher from England who is here for the summer, and we have been working on a bi-centennial programme in which we looked at five parts of American history--the Mechlenburg Declaration, The Declaration of Independence (we helped Mr. Jefferson to draft it), the freeing of slaves, the first flight of the Wright Brothers, and finally the resignation of Mr. Nixon. After this, we had the idea that we should make a national monument to commemorate the bi-centennial, and we decided that it should be in four parts--something which celebrates the known past, for historians; something to represent the hidden past, the archaelogists; something to represent the at present unknown, for the scientists; and lastly something which represents the at-present incomplete--the common man. So we need a block of land somewhere in the Eastern part of America to have it built.

On a separate sheet, we have listed all the things we think are important to remember about museums.

We hope you will send us a reply with your comments.

Yours sincerely,

Mrs. Heathcote's Class at
Mount Tabor.

*****

Dear MR. President:

We are Mrs. Heathcote's drama class from Winston-Salem - we are 4th & 5th grade. We would like you to set aside a block of land for a monument -, we think it should be in Philadelphia or Winston-Salem.

Lisa Taylor

Tammy Lee	Jon Haire
Toni Brandon	Becki Meyer
Sara Carter	Ruth Ellen Hargen
Richard McCurdy	Jan Coward
Missie Hughes	Pam McHone
Mary K. James	Michele McGrail
Wade Albreath	Marianne Heathcote.

*****

Things we believe are important in museums ... and especially for the one we would like to build if we ever could.

1. We expect history to be confusing because it is.
2. We want things people have made in it.
3. We want to have an opportunity to use our own imagination before guides start to tell us about it.
4. People who come should enjoy it and not be told everything first.
5. Guides should help people understand but NOT TELL. Guides can answer questions.
6. The museum should show in some way the two faces of science--the good and the bad.
7. Museums should make people more curious--not less.
8. Museums should reveal how people lived not just show.
9. Museums should make you remember the past.
10. The museum should never be finished, and people who visit should also do a bit of work in it--or at it.
11. There should be something in the museum which makes you want to tell other people about it.
12. We should want to keep coming back to it, so we must never see everything at once.

13. We should enjoy the past.
14. The museum should contain experiences which make us constantly compare the past and the present.
15. The museum should keep adding the past that keeps coming.

*****

THE WHITE HOUSE

WASHINGTON

August 14, 1975

Dear Mrs. Heathcote:

On behalf of President Ford, I would like to take this opportunity to thank you for your letter and your students for their letter in reference to the Bicentennial.

The ideas of your students for a museum show much thought and creativity.

Unfortunately, due to the heavy demands on the President's time and the multitude of similar requests, he is unable to send a personal message as he would like to. Therefore, I am enclosing an inscribed photograph to Wake Forest University and a message the President put together in an attempt to express his appreciation for the efforts of so many people such as you and your students to make our Bicentennial celebration one to remember.

Thank you again for taking your time to write and best of wishes for the Bicentennial era.

Sincerely,

Milton E. Mitler
Deputy Special Assistant
to the President

*****

THE WHITE HOUSE

WASHINGTON

I warmly commend all who participate in plans for the celebration of our National Bicentennial. Your efforts are symbolic of your deep sense of patriotism and civic pride. They also reflect the vitality and spirit of America.

I wholeheartedly welcome your commitment to make our Nation's two hundredth birthday a fitting and memorable occasion for all of us.

Gerald R. Ford

EDUCATIONAL DRAMA AND THE CREATIVE PROCESS

R. Baird Shuman

At the center of everything connected with school is a child who is acting out for a major part of his first 16, 17, or 18 years of life the dramatic stuff of which his entire future is likely to be composed. His acquiescence or disobedience, his convergence to or divergence from behavioral norms, his happiness or sadness, his activity or passivity, his gregariousness or isolation, his acceptance or rejection, his self-esteem or self-hate, his success or failure, his ease in learning or difficulty in learning will all determine what he will become, what he will contribute to his society, what satisfactions he will gain from having lived, and what ultimately the world will become, since the world is made up of hundreds of millions of people who are shaped as much by what happens to them in their formative years as they are by heredity. Because, in developed countries, schools reach all children for substantial periods during these formative years, the questions of what and how to teach them are awesomely important. The course of society, in a very real way, depends upon the answers to these questions.

CREATIVITY AND EDUCATION

Today's Schools

Schools in the United States can generally be said to be quite rigidly organized, formalistic, subject- more than student-oriented.[1] Essentially they reward, in both teachers and students, convergent thinking more than divergent thinking, acceptance more than questioning, passivity more than activity, consensus more than dissent.

Irwin Flescher, a researcher in the area of creativity,

questions why "original thinking should be expected to be a relevant factor in scholastic achievement, the nature of [scholastic achievement] being so markedly convergent in content. Formal learning is very unlike original and creative activity, and convincing evidence of a significant relationship is still wanting."[2] Getzels and Jackson report findings which tend to support Flescher's contention. In their random sampling of some 449 students from a private secondary school in the Midwest, they found that "subjects at the top 20 percent on the creativity measures when compared with the same-sex age peers [were] below the top 20 percent in IQ. Their mean IQ was 127, with a range from 108 to 138.... [But] subjects in the top 20 percent in IQ when compared with same-sex peers [were] below the top 20 percent on the creativity measures. Their mean IQ was 150, with a range from 139 to 179."[3] These findings, while perhaps not conclusive, are strongly suggestive: the creative youngster's creative potential is not necessarily matched by his academic achievement nor suggested by it.

Identifying the Creative Child

Many teachers--and, for that matter, parents--do not know how to identify the child with great creative potential. Before the creativity of such a child has blossomed, those who judge creativity by end products such as paintings or poems may not know what the early signs of creativity are and may misread these early signs in such extreme ways as to suspect retardation rather than creative potential. Morris I. Stein cautions, "Often, in studying creativity, we tend to restrict ourselves to a study of the genius because the 'distance' between what he has done and what has existed is quite marked. Such an approach causes us to overlook a necessary distinction between the creative product and the creative experience. The child who fixes the bell on his tricycle for the first time may go through stages that are structurally similar to those which characterize the work of the genius."[4]

The potentially creative child may be much out of step with his peers. He probably will be the child with different--and perhaps seemingly incorrect--perceptions of what exists around him. He may be the child who does not keep pace with the rest of the class. He may be like the teacher described by Sylvia Ashton-Warner in Spinster who became so completely absorbed in the discovery of a new method of teaching her students to read that she exclaimed, "I am utterly lost in the present!" Paul Torrance suggests that "intense absorption in listening, observing, doing" and "losing awareness of time"[5] are often indications of creative potential in youngsters; yet, ironically, these are characteristics which would not endear students to a good many teachers, because they would make the student seem out of step with the rest of the class.

Among other characteristics of creative potential which the child may manifest, Torrance lists, "Using analogies in speech and writing; bodily involvement in writing, reading and drawing; ... eagerness to tell others about discoveries; continued creative work after 'time is up'; tendency to show relationships among apparently unrelated ideas; ... imaginative play; ... habit of guessing outcomes and checking accuracy; ... [and] manipulation of objects and ideas to obtain new combinations."[6] All of these characteristics suggest behaviors that the teacher wishing to use educational drama in the classroom might turn to excellent advantage.

How to Encourage the Child's Creativity

Any child's creativity waxes or wanes, depending largely upon the environment in which he finds himself. The family environment is of considerable importance[7]; however, the school environment may be of even more importance, because the typical student in school may find himself initially in a more threatening environment than he has experienced at home. If a climate of trust is not built within the school environment, the child may turn inward and his developing creativity may never emerge so fully as it would in an environment of trust and security.[8]

Torrance reminds teachers that if they wish to move in the direction of encouraging more creative development in their students, they must ask themselves some searching questions:

Would you be willing to let your pupils ask questions about whatever puzzles them?

Would you teach something outside your prepared lessons?

Would you teach something outside the curriculum approved by your school or school system?

Would you permit a child to work alone in the classroom?

Would you permit a child to continue an activity in which he is absorbed, even if he has to miss a planned activity?

Would you recognize and acknowledge some heretofore unrecognized potential and give it a chance to develop, even if the child misbehaves a great deal?

Would you allow the child to be successful in some way that is possible for him, even though it is not the way you had planned?

Would you withhold criticism or correction long enough to permit a child to discover and correct his own errors?

Would you give the unliked and unloved child a chance to make constructive contributions to the welfare of the group?

Would you sometimes carry out a child's ideas about a classroom activity?

Would you encourage, permit, and give credit for self-initiated learning inside and outside the classroom?

Would you use fantasies to help children get at real problems?

Would you support a child against peer pressures to conformity against his convictions?

Would you respect and acknowledge the potentialities of slow learners?

Would you plan a lesson specifically to help one child solve a problem?[9]

It is vital that teachers continually ask themselves questions that will help them achieve an honest view of how far they can go as teachers without feeling uncomfortable. Teachers who have defined their own limits often do well to work within those limits. This is not to say that they should not seek to expand their limits as they continue to grow within their own careers. But if teachers realize, for example, that they are not comfortable in permitting children to miss planned activities in order to finish something they are doing, it is well that this limitation be acknowledged in advance, because it is better for teachers to set down clearly defined rules that are consistently enforced rather than to explode at students when the teachers' patience has been tried beyond their level of tolerance.

Those who are dedicated to encouraging creativity may have to move slowly in that direction. They will, in moving toward greater creativity, make additional work for themselves, and they must face realistically and honestly the question whether they can carry this extra burden. They may find that they receive little or no support from colleagues, administrators, and the community, so they must ask themselves whether they can function productively in a situation in which such support is not present. Margaret Mead speaks to this point: "The teacher, however deep her commitment is to her subject matter and to bringing out unusual gifts, cannot risk bringing out gifts that may disrupt the precarious balance of her overcrowded classroom. Under today's conditions, the best teacher has little time or energy for any kind of creativity, and none for the disruptive sort."[10] However, Mead, by implication, places subject matter at the center of the learning situation rather than the student. The teacher who truly feels that the student occupies the central position will usually find a means of dealing with him or her in such a way as to engage the child's creativity.

Risk-Taking

Productive creative development involves students in taking considerable risks. American students are not often encouraged to take risks. Torrance asserts, "The United States has frequently been characterized as the most success-oriented culture in the world. Our education is said to prepare only for success, not for coping with frustration and failure. Frustration and failure must be avoided either by succeeding or not attempting ventures where failure is a possibility." Torrance goes on to say, "Success orientation, when greatly overemphasized, is inimical to creative growth because creative ways of learning involve experimentation, taking risks, making mistakes and correcting them."[11]

While the schools are putting a high premium on "right" answers and convergent behavior, parents are often looking for the high grade--and this is usually earned through "right" answers and convergent behavior. At the same time, peer pressures are building. According to Torrance, "young people are more concerned about the evaluations of peers than of parents, teachers, and other authorities.... Original ideas are common targets of peer pressures to conformity."[12]

Keeping Alive the Dream

Daydreaming is antithetical to most of the linear, convergent types of activities and learning patterns that comprise the curriculum in the average school. Most education from grade one through graduate school is aimed at taming the emotions, disciplining the mind. And this emphasis can be death to the creative urge in youngsters. Arthur Koestler observes, "The laws of disciplined thinking demand that we should stick to a given frame of reference and not shift from one universe of discourse to another.... But when concentration flags and primitive motivations take over, thought will shift from one matrix to another, like a ball bouncing down a mountain stream, each time an idea ... provides a link to a more attractive context."[13] And it is precisely in these leaps of both the conscious and subconscious mind that man's creative power is stimulated and honed.

The school can quite easily provide a setting in which the mind is encouraged to make leaps from matrix to matrix, but such activity is often misunderstood and dismissed as being non-essential, and an individual child's reveries and daydreams are the subject of scolding rather than rejoicing. And it is probably this fact more than any other that encourages peer pressures which come to be directed against the creative child, the original thinker. "Creativity in its widest sense is not only the function of an individual but of a group as well--an actualization of surplus potentials, of capacities which are untapped or dormant under ordinary conditions, but which, under exceptional circumstances, reveal themselves in original forms of behavior."[14]

As youngsters progress through today's schools, many of their dreams are interrupted, scorned, and in many cases shattered. And this is not surprising in light of the fact that most teachers in contemporary schools are dealing with such large numbers that they feel constrained from risking situations which might move quickly beyond their ability to control them. Elizabeth Drews, who believes that most secondary schools and higher institutions inhibit students' curiosity and reduce their motivation for further learning, calls for a new kind of teacher, in effect a teacher-counselor-consultant who would function as a facilitator of learning and who would guide students toward an active involvement in the learning environment, steering them into experiences which would, in highly individualized ways, involve them in group discussion, independent study, the development of social conscience and aesthetic appreciation, and use of resources rather than dependence on a curriculum.[15] Drews would free the student to grow in creativity and, in the Brunerian sense, through discovery to become acquainted with those learning structures which make learning an independent and lifelong possibility.

EDUCATIONAL DRAMA AS A MEANS OF NURTURING CREATIVITY

Educational Drama Defined

Dorothy Heathcote, one of the most renowned exponents of education drama, is more concerned with drama as a system than as a subject. For her purposes, she defines educational drama as "anything which involves persons in active role-taking situations in which attitudes, not characters, are the chief concern."[16] Nellie McCaslin defines it (using the phrase "creative drama") as "the play that is developed by a group, as opposed to the one that abides by a written script."[17] Creative drama involves essentially a composing process demanding independent thinking and encouraging the child's creative processes. Although it is generally a group activity, a creative drama "is composed of the contributions of each individual, and every contribution is important. As the group plans together, each member is encouraged to express his own ideas and thereby contribute to the whole. The leader recognizes the part each child plays, and the value that planning has for him."[18] Children who cannot compose easily on paper usually become so quickly involved in the forward thrust of the drama which they and their fellow students are making that, caught up in the tension of the situation, they compose freely and act their parts naturally.

The Role of the Teacher in Educational Drama

In any teaching situation and in the employment of any teaching technique, the teacher, sensitive to the subtle and not-so-subtle messages that the group is sending, aware of the nuances of the group and the situation, and realistically cognizant of his or her own limitations within a given classroom environment, will constantly be defining and redefining the teacher's role. This role may be defined in terms of immediate and mundane considerations: "I have a miserable cold today, so I must try to spare my voice"; "These kids did not cooperate yesterday, so I must work on getting them to function better in the group situation"; "It is beastly hot, so we will try not to move around too much"; or "My principal, who likes things to be orderly and quiet, is showing visitors around the school this morning." These are all typical of matters which enter into teachers' role definitions for a given day.

On a broader basis, teachers need to define their roles in terms of what Heathcote calls their "thresholds," for if these thresholds are undefined or ill-defined--that is, if teachers do not know themselves well enough to realize their own tolerances--activities may be started which the teacher cannot see through or allow to continue to their logical conclusions. Heathcote identifies seven thresholds or registers which can affect a teacher's performance markedly: the noise threshold, the space threshold, the group-size threshold, the decision-threshold, the threshold of the teacher's subject interests, the evaluation and standards thresholds, and the variety of teaching registers the teacher may use in day-to-day confrontations.[19]

The thresholds which teachers must be particularly aware of if they are to embark on activities in educational drama are the noise and space thresholds. Teachers must ask themselves not only how much noise and disorder they can stand, but how much can be permitted before teachers and students in nearby rooms are disturbed or before school administrators lodge complaints. These are practical considerations which every teacher will need to take into account before involving students in any activity that might press toward the upper limit of these thresholds. Some teachers may wish to proceed as Herbert Kohl suggests and take the consequences: "If a particular teacher becomes threatening and your supervisors also disapprove of noise then you may be able to find a way to calm the teacher down and negotiate a truce. Perhaps you can find that teacher's weakness and complain about it, instead of being defensive about the noise in one's own room."[20]

It is essential that teachers (1) know their thresholds and (2) strive consciously to extend these thresholds. But teachers whose students push them beyond their thresholds may react arbitrarily and emotionally, possibly destroying an ongoing situation which might have led to a desirable creative outcome for the students. Kohl, who recommends that teachers be themselves, warns very sagely, "One ought not to try something basically incompatible with one's personality. It is likely to cause frustration and hostility, and to make further experimentation seem more dangerous than it really is."[21] These words must be heeded by the teacher who is in the initial throes of role definition and particularly by the teacher who wishes to use educational drama as a means of learning.

Working toward Improvisation

Although improvisation is a rather natural occurrence in the normal play activities of pre-school and primary students who usually fantasize and compose easily and with great originality, the inhibitions which cause a decline in student creativity around fourth grade and again around seventh grade[22] are generally sufficiently strong that children beyond the third grade need to be led toward improvisation by gradual steps. Even though pre-school and primary youngsters improvise easily, some of their teachers will find a greater security in pre-improvisational activities than they would be able to experience if they plunged immediately into improvisation. If such is the case, teachers should do what makes them feel most confident and relaxed because if teachers are tense and dissatisfied with an activity, it is a sure bet that the students will not be gaining much from pursuing it.

Warm-Up Activities

Warm-up activities are designed essentially to make students aware of the communicative potential of their bodies. Most warm-up activities will be non-verbal and some may be in the form of guessing games similar to charades. Through these exercises, students gain a oneness with the group and their inhibitions gradually melt away. Such activities, although they may be repeated several times over a number of days or even weeks, should not run for more than ten or fifteen minutes at any one time. They should be concluded while the students are still eager for more of them.

Many warm-up activities involve pairs of students in situations like the following:

Mirroring: Face your partner. Pretend to put a contact lens into your right eye. Your partner will perform the mirrored act, working in reverse.[23]

Sculpting: You are a mound of clay. Your partner is a sculptor. Take form as your partner molds you.

Exclusion: All the students form a circle, excluding just one student. Join hands and keep him or her from getting in or out. Play this at least seven or eight times so that no one student will feel rejected personally.

Tug-of-War: Divide the students into two equal groups and have a tug-of-war with an imaginary rope.

Strength: Face your partner. Press the palms of your hands against the palms of your partner's hands and push as hard as you can, seeing who can hold out the longest.

Observing: Place 25-30 commonplace objects on a table. Divide the class into teams. Have one student from Team A and one from Team B look at the table for 20 seconds. Then have them turn away. Remove three or four items. Have both students write on a pad what has been removed. The first one to list all the missing items scores for his team.[24]

These activities, undertaken early, place few verbal demands upon students. They enjoy performing and they free themselves up for those more complicated activities which will come later.

Body Movement Exercises

At all stages of educational dramatic activities, students should use body movement exercises to limber up and to keep discovering new means of non-verbal communication. Some valuable exercises involving body movement are easy to employ:

You are confined to a small space bubble with zero gravity. You are nearing a distant planet. You need to photograph as much of it as you can. Do so.

On the phonograph play Debussy's Nuages, Ravel's Bolero, or Grieg's Peer Gynt. Invite students to react with their bodies to what they hear. Now try it with Hawaiian or Indian or Chinese music.

On a slide projector, show the students a slide of a picture like Wyeth's Christina's World or a picture from Edward Steichen's The Family of Man. Invite each student individually to move as the picture directs him or her to.

You are an acorn resting in the earth. As moisture and warmth reach you, you sprout. Now you reach above the earth. Now you become a slender trunk. Now you grow taller, and taller, and taller. Now you produce branches and leaves.

Read the students a brief action poem and have them move to it.

Many activities of this sort will suggest themselves. Students may devise some. Just as scales and finger exercises are necessary to the serious pianist, body movement exercises regularly engaged in are necessary to students participating in a program of educational drama.

Pantomime

Pantomime--or mime, as it is often designated--is interpretive, nonverbal acting. Its most noted exponents of late have been Charlie Chaplin and Marcel Marceau. Following activities like those suggested above, pantomime can lead students one step further in developing a sensitivity to body movement and its dramatic possibilities. Exercises in mime can be used much as the warm-up activities above were. They shouldn't involve time spans of more than ten or fifteen minutes. They can involve a competitive element, although they need not. The following very simple pantomime activities should be done with no props, and it is essential that they remain non-verbal:

Wash an imaginary window.
Butter a very hot muffin.
Wind a clock.
Replace a light bulb.
Butter and eat an ear of corn.

Frost a three-layer cake.

Walk as though you had a stone in the heel of your left shoe.

Catch a butterfly in a butterfly net.[25]

These pantomimes, each taking no more than a minute or two, should be played as charades, with students guessing what is being depicted. They should be followed by more interpretive pantomimes, such as the following:

Students are given words on cards. They come before the class and act out their words while the class guesses the word they are acting out.

The class gathers in the center of the room and greets other members of the class, using no words but relying on handshakes, gestures and eye contact for meaning.

A student crosses a stream by walking from rock to rock until the far bank is reached.

Three or four members of the class come to a central position and act out the following: "You receive a telegram. You are expected to hear that you have been offered a new job, but instead you are told to report for an army physical." "No one appreciates me!" "If you say that again, I'll punch you!" "Can't you see I'm a pedestrian?"

Act out the following: You are accused of a crime that you did not commit. Defend yourself.

You are trapped in something and are trying to escape. Have the class guess what it is you are trapped in.

(Three participants). You have been hurt in the wilderness. Two people carry you to a point from which help can be summoned.[26]

Other mimes can be generated from having students look at pictures of people and act out the characters they see in the pictures. Or they might take an action, such as driving a car, and perform it like a teen-aged hot-rodder, a middle-aged salesman driving home after a week on the road, a 78-year-old widow driving home from the supermarket in heavy traffic, a drunk driving home from a party, a policeman driving in pursuit of a drunk driving home from a party.

Miming will cause the participants to interpret roles and to project characters convincingly. It emphasizes movement and non-verbal reaction to stipulated situations. Students engage enthusiastically in miming. The situation is low-risk for most of them, yet through it they gain the confidence they will need in the higher-risk situation of improvisation.

Role Playing

Role-playing activities demand improvisation, yet they are, like warm-up activities and pantomiming, usually created by teachers whose control of the situation is felt because they have originated it. Teachers who feel that they must originate and direct activities will usually feel quite comfortable in using such activities. If they build up to role playing, they will have communicated to their students what they will and will not tolerate in the classroom.

In role playing, students must assume a predetermined role and create dialog as they go along. Simulation games depend upon the techniques of role playing, and some teachers find it useful to resort to the use of such games, since they are often well designed and intricately worked out. Games can be closely related to play activities, in which youngsters so naturally engage on their own, except that in the game, participants have certain stated objectives and must work within the framework of achieving those objectives.[27]

If games and role playing are used with classes, it is desirable to involve every student. If half the class plays while half watches, those watching will likely stimulate from some of the players reactions that will cause them to slip out of character. If everyone is intensely involved, this does not happen. The teacher at the beginning of the activity needs to say something like, "In order to make our play believable, everyone must act as the character he is portraying would really act in the situation being depicted. If anyone falls out of character, he may risk destroying our play, and we would not like that to happen, would we?" Taking a cue from a memorable improvisation conducted by Dorothy Heathcote in Asheville, North Carolina, in June 1975, I always tell youngsters, "It is perfectly natural that you may feel peculiar and may come close to slipping out of character. If this happens, try to control yourself, but if you cannot, just step aside and leave the play for a short time. Come back when you are again able to participate. We will go on without you if this happens."

Mrs. Heathcote had created a tense situation. Slaves who had been brought into a courtyard had just been told that if they did not all accept the god of the sun within one day, Pharoah would have them executed. There were two holdouts, and the other slaves gathered around to convince them, as Pharoah's soldiers were sealing the well so that the slaves could not drink. A small girl giggled. Heathcote approached her and said, "It is perfectly understandable that you giggled, but the slave you are playing would not be giggling now. Would you mind stepping aside until you have controlled your giggle?" Just as the girl was stepping aside, another girl giggled. Heathcote said, "You see, what I said was true. Someone else has giggled. Would you step aside, too?" Then Heathcote asked, "Does anyone else feel in danger of giggling?" A boy, barely able to control himself, allowed, "Yes, ma'm." And at this point, Heathcote's genius with youngsters showed. She said, 'Well, you step aside, too, will you? And since there are three of you, now, would you mind guarding the well? Just stand there with your backs to each other and see that no one tries to break into it." The students assumed their places, stationed so that they could not see each other's faces, and fell easily and quite seriously into their new roles. As they grew interested in the forward action of the improvisation, they, one by one, slipped back into their old characters and resumed their participation.

The "Air Raid Shelter" simulation works quite well with secondary school youngsters and forces them to consider quite seriously what their value systems are. The situation:

> You and twenty-six other people are in an air raid shelter after a major nuclear attack. You do not know what conditions are like outside. You know that you must remain in the shelter for twenty days in order to avoid contamination. But there are food and water for only twelve people for that length of time. Fifteen people must be placed in a holding chamber to face almost certain death. You may be the only people left on the planet, so it is important that those who remain can cope with the conditions they might find outside and that they be capable of beginning the repopulation of the planet if necessary.

The cast of characters is presented in specific detail: "Joan

Pearson, 46, Phi Beta Kappa, Vassar. Pulitzer Prize in Journalism. Divorced. No children." "Peter O'Malley, 27, recently-ordained Roman Catholic priest. Knows Latin, Greek, and Hebrew. Likes to garden. Was raised on a farm. Good mechanical ability." "Jenny Jones, 16, unmarried, 4 months pregnant. School drop-out. Severe reading problems. Antagonistic to authority figures. Good cook." The cast of characters should include nurses, doctors, mechanics, and other people with specified skills. Some of the most skilled people should be past 60 years old.

Given this basic situation, students have little difficulty generating convincing dialogue. They improvise easily having been given the initial push toward doing so.

A variation on this is to provide for a free improvisation, but to assign one role. Place a student at a table on which is a sign reading, "Francis Chadwick, Mayor" or "Lillian Medfield, M.D." When one such role is assigned, a framework is suggested for an improvisation, and this suggestion can help students to get started.

Open-Ended Stories

Another device that teachers will find useful in moving students toward improvisation is the open-ended story. The teacher reads a story up to a certain crucial point and then invites the students to act out an ending, improvising as they proceed. Any exciting story that students enjoy will serve the purpose here, and the improvisation which ensues will lead students to significant gains in values clarification. Some teachers may wish to compose their own open-ended stories. Others may wish to read an anthologized story up to the crucial point. Yet others may find Milton Velder and Edwin Cohen's _Open-Ended Stories_ (New York: Globe, 1973) a useful resource.

Improvisation

Improvisation differs from the educational drama techniques cited above in that at its most successful level, it is almost totally student-centered and student-planned rather than teacher-centered and teacher-planned. Improvisation cannot succeed if it carries the teacher far beyond the thresholds or tolerances that Heathcote has identified. Charles Duke cautions, "The teacher's approach to creative dramatics is bound to depend on his attitude toward discipline. If the teacher angers easily, cannot accept criticism, blows up if things go awry, demands immediate results or doesn't have the patience to let people move as rapidly or as slowly as they wish, and does not believe in introducing democratic procedures into the classroom, then he will not want to utilize creative dramatics in his teaching. Nothing is so good for children as a good dramatic experience--and nothing is so bad as a bad one."[28]

The major purpose of improvisation is not that of producing a measurable outcome in the form of a play--although such an outcome may result from the activity. The essential purpose is that of getting youngsters to experience something outside their normal realms of experience.

Teachers must work skillfully to see that this opportunity is not foreclosed to the student, and this means that teachers must keep in mind continually the major purpose of what they are doing.

Two examples from Heathcote will serve to illustrate this point. In her film Three Looms Waiting, one group of boys have decided that they wish to play a prisoner-of-war scene to be set in Germany during World War II. Heathcote says, 'You prisoners will have to get your characters down because your keepers are going to grill you." She then turns to one lad and begins grilling him: "Is your mother alive? What does she do? Where does she live? Is your father alive? What did he do before he died?" etc. At one point she asks the boy, "Where do you come from?" "London," he responds. "Where in London?" she counters. "Coventry," he answers.

In the analysis following the film, Heathcote is asked why she did not tell the boy that Coventry is not a part of London. She answers, "I don't give a damn where Coventry is!" She wisely realizes that she is not engaged here in giving a geography lesson but rather in getting a young student to know what it feels like to be a prisoner in a foreign land and to respond to the emotions which this feeling engenders. To have provided the geographical correction here would have been to destroy the moment, to have retarded the very process which she was at that moment seeking to build. She would have proved only one thing: I know more than you. And this is the very thing that the skillful teacher will not wish to emphasize at this critical point in the development of the situation.

In Dorothy Heathcote Talks to Teachers, Heathcote tells of being faced with another difficult problem: During an improvisation, the tiniest boy in the room wished to play the monster. Obviously, his size made him seem unqualified for the role; however, his desire to play it was genuine--and wholly understandable psychologically. Heathcote's task as an effective teacher was to find a means of allowing the student to satisfy his desire. Since he could not look like a convincing monster, she decided to find out whether he might sound like one. She asked him how loudly and frighteningly he could roar and having ascertained that he could, indeed, sound like the most monstrous of monsters, she had him hide behind a wall, roaring his heart out and quite convincingly frightening the other participants in the drama. And this tiny boy, who probably had often been frightened but had never been very frightening to others came to feel what it was like to be the frightener rather than the frightenee.

In proceeding toward improvisation, teachers facilitate the situation by asking questions, but they do not suggest any preferences they might have. They might start things moving by asking, "Do you want your drama to be in the here-and-now or at some time in the past?" The students then talk this out among themselves, working toward the sort of consensus about when and where the drama will be set that will permit them to proceed to the question of what the drama will be about. But throughout this process, the teacher is much in the background, preferably apart from the group, eavesdropping, but not participating. And this early stage cannot be rushed. It must be talked out in full if it is to lead the students to the next logical step, that of narrowing down the time, the locus, the plot, the characterization. The teacher may be invited to play a part in the drama, but this decision must rest with the students. If they do not invite the teacher to assume a role, then the teacher must be willing to be a spectator.

As the students are leading into the drama, the teacher may help to sharpen the focus by asking questions, but these questions should be asked honestly--that is, a desired answer should be implied neither by the question nor by the manner in which it is asked.

Teachers often worry about their ability and the ability of their students to handle a chosen topic. Suppose the students want to do a drama about Japan. Do they know enough about Japan to carry the drama through to its conclusion?

Ask yourself, "What do I know about Japan?" If you can list eight or ten things you know about Japan, you have enough for a beginning drama. My list includes the following factual items: Made up of many islands; cherry trees; kimonos; dependent on the sea for food and employment; geographically small; of volcanic origins; has an emperor; delicacy in written expression--the haiku; value ability to arrange flowers; sleep on mats on the floor; tea is an important ceremony; honor is very important to the Japanese. This list would provide enough information that a play could be generated, _provided that the teacher remembers that the purpose is not to teach about Japan per se_, but rather to provide the opportunity for the students to experience some aspect of that culture by living through it as a character in a drama. If the play is carried on for a week or two, as some educational dramas will be, students might wish to do library study on Japan. If the drama runs its course in a day, its purpose has been served and any factual inaccuracies need not be worried about excessively.

If students have great difficulty in getting started--and some groups are bound to--two suggestions by Nellie McCaslin may prove useful.[29] One might be just to provide the students with some props--an old radio, a pair of broken eye-glasses, theater stubs, a sponge--and let them devise a play in which all of the props are used in some prominent way. Or the teacher might bring in a box of costumes--old hats, sweaters, jackets, etc.--and allow students to select one or more pieces of clothing to wear in the play. The play will quite easily be generated from such a situation.

Drama and Creativity

Educational drama demands that participants invent. Students do not feel the fear of failing that they often experience in other school situations. Drama and play are closely related, and students fall naturally into both. And in so doing, they are able to exercise all of their creative powers and, indeed, build these powers consistently, confidently, and positively. Civilizations are best remembered for the creative activities of those people who helped to build them. If schools do not nurture creativity above all else, civilization cannot move forward.

References

[1]Perhaps the most convincing evidence regarding this characterization is to be found in Charles E. Silberman's Crisis in the Classroom (New York: Random House, 1970), or in the two reports of the Anglo-American Conference on the Teaching of English held at Dartmouth College in 1966, John Dixon's Growth through English, 2nd ed. (London: Oxford University Press, 1969) and Herbert J. Muller's The Uses of English (New York: Holt, Rinehart, & Winston, 1967).

[2]"Anxiety and Achievement of Intellectually Gifted and Creatively Gifted Children," Journal of Psychology 56 (1963), 265.

[3]"Family Environment and Cognitive Style: A Study of the Sources of Highly Intelligent and of Highly Creative Adolescents," American Sociological Review 26 (1961), 352-353.

[4]"Creativity and Culture," in Ross L. Mooney and Taher A. Razik, eds., Explorations in Creativity (New York: Harper and Row, 1967), pp. 109-110.

[5]"Nurture of Creative Talents," in Mooney and Razik, op. cit., p. 190. See also his "Creative Abilities of Elementary School Children," in William B. Michael, ed., Teaching for Creative Endeavor: Bold New Venture (Bloomington: Indiana University Press, 1968), pp. 20-21.

[6]Torrance in Teaching for Creative Endeavor, p. 21.

[7]See the Getzels and Jackson article, reference 3.

[8]A useful research report on the topic of the effect of environment upon creativity is found in Paul S. Weisberg and Kayla J. Springer's "Environmental Factors in Creative Function," Archives of General Psychiatry 5 (December 1961), 64-74.

[9]Torrance in Teaching for Creative Endeavor, pp. 5-6.

[10]"Where Education Fits In," Think, November-December 1962, p. 19.

[11]Torrance in Explorations in Creativity, p. 187.

[12]Ibid., p. 187.

[13]The Act of Creation (New York: Macmillan, 1964), p. 178.

[14]Catherine Jones, "The Creativity Problem," Illinois Schools Journal 51 (Spring 1971), 2.

[15]"Fernwood: A Free School," Journal of Humanistic Psychology 8 (1968), 113-122.

[16]"Drama and Education: Subject or System?" in Nigel Dodd and Winifred Hickson, eds., Drama and Theatre in Education (London: Heinemann, 1973), p. 43.

[17]Creative Dramatics in the Classroom (New York: McKay, 1968), p. 8.

[18]Ibid., p. 11.

[19]Heathcote in Drama and Theatre in Education; see also her "How Does Drama Serve Thinking, Talking, and Writing?" Elementary English 47 (December 1970), 1080.

[20]The Open Classroom: A Practical Guide to a New Way of Teaching (New York: New York Review Books, 1969), p. 84.

[21]Ibid., p. [69].

[22]Torrance in Explorations in Creativity, p. 187.

[23]Charles R. Duke discusses the use of this technique in "Drama," in R. Baird Shuman, ed., Creative Approaches to the Teaching of English: Secondary (Itasca, Ill.: F. E. Peacock, 1974).

[24]Some of these warm-up activities are adapted from Aaron Hillman's "The Play's the Thing," in George Isaac Brown, ed., The Live Classroom (New York: Viking Press, 1975), pp. 276-291, passim.

[25]Some of these activities are adapted from R. Baird Shuman's "Drama in the Schools: A Wellspring of Creativity," Journal of English Teaching Techniques 5 (winter 1972-3), 18-19.

[26] Suggested by Hillman, in Brown's The Live Classroom, pp. 277ff.

[27] Roger Caillois, Man, Play and Games (New York: Free Press, 1961), pp. 3-10. See also James S. Colemen, "The Role of Modern Technology in Relation to Simulation and Games for Learning," Academy for Educational Development, Washington, D. C., 1970; ERIC: ED 139 704.

[28] Creative Dramatics and English Teaching (Urbana, Ill.: NCTE, 1974), p. 68.

[29] Creative Dramatics in the Classroom, pp. 51-54.

EDUCATIONAL DRAMA, ROLE-TAKING, AND VALUES CLARIFICATION

Charles R. Duke

"I just can't do it."

"What do you mean?"

"Oh, you know, that role-playing jazz the hot-shot consultant advised us to use in our classrooms. I tried it and the kids went wild. I mean, we were studying Steinbeck's The Pearl, and we had fifteen minutes left in the period so I asked them how'd they like to do something different. Naturally, they said yes, so I told them to pick any two characters in the novel and role play a scene."

"So, what happened? Didn't they do it?"

"Do it? They just sat there and looked at me and then wanted to know how they should go about playing a scene and what scene should they use. By the time I had told them what to do, the time was gone and the bell rang for the end of the period."

"Well, maybe you need to plan the role playing a little more."

"Nope, I've had it; takes too much effort and, besides, I never was any good at acting. You can try it if you want to, but let me have my regular routine any day. At least the kids know what is expected of them."

Conversations such as this one occur in teachers' lounges all over the country. Although the specific complaint may vary, the result is often the same. Teachers still shy away from role playing because they do not understand its purpose, nor have they been sufficiently trained in its many uses. Almost every education methods text contains a short section on the value of role playing as an instructional strategy, but the usefulness of the approach never seems to be stressed adequately nor is its appropriateness to a variety of subject matter sufficiently understood.[1]

APPROACHES TO ROLE PLAYING

Definitions

A number of definitions can be offered to show what role playing may be. For example, role playing allows an individual to take the part of another and try to act and respond as though the individual were that person. Or we can consider role playing in a larger context. According to Fannie and George Shaftel, it is a group problem-solving method that enables people to explore in spontaneous drama how they expect to solve certain problems, what alternatives are available to them, and what personal and social consequences the proposed solutions will provide.[2] All role playing relies on the spontaneous performance of participants when they have been placed in a hypothetical situation. The essential core of the activity is understanding the situation of another person, but what may happen in a role play is anyone's guess; that is, there are no formal restraints on a situation, even if the group involved may be aware of some general objectives toward which they might work.

The act of role playing involves a fairly complex process; it does not consist simply of starting in and doing anything that comes to mind. Effective role playing instead focuses upon handling data--details and issues which lead to a definition of a problem; tentative decision-making in the choosing among alternatives of action; experiencing the consequences of these choices--going through the dramatizations in which various choices are tested for appropriateness; and making final decisions. This kind of activity is reality-centered. The individual is placed in a position where the opportunity to feel what is at stake occurs; then comes the experience of relating the situation to the differing situations of others. When it is properly used, role playing permits the kind of discovery learning which occurs when individuals in a group face up to the ways they tend to solve their problems of interpersonal relations while becoming conscious of personal value systems.[3]

Through effective role playing, then, students gain a greater understanding of other roles and relationships as well as a better awareness of what they themselves are doing. The resulting values of role playing are many:

A development of increased self-understanding and an awareness of personal feelings

A way of releasing feelings safely

A development of empathy for and insight into other people and their situations

A way for trying out new behaviors and experimenting with new roles

A development of skills for group problem-solving

An opportunity for learning and practicing new social skills

An improvement of psychomotor skills

A way to foster creativity and imagination

An enhancement for subject matter learning.[4]

Attitudes toward Role Playing

The most common error in trying to introduce role playing into the classroom is attempting to do too much too soon before adequate preparation for the experience. Not too surprisingly, role playing presents considerable risks for the older student. Young children are less likely to find it difficult to slip in and out of roles, make physical contact with each other, and, in general, practice a "willing suspension of disbelief." The older student, however, tends to be inhibited. The thought of having to become someone else, to act as if the role were real, presents a frightening challenge to some adolescents. Caught up in their own personal identity crises, hypersensitive to their images with classmates, and still uncertain of what constitutes "proper" behavior in various situations, adolescents may well refuse to take part in role playing if thrust into it without preparation.

For role playing to be successful, students must be free to respond with flexibility and to allow enactments to evolve organically rather than mechanically. The mechanical aspects stressed by many teachers doom role playing to failure. Therefore, to prepare students for effective role playing, a sequence should be followed that will lead gradually to fully developed enactments which allow students to role play without self-consciousness or fear and which are organic in nature.

The process leading to role playing divides naturally into three steps or stages: (1) students become acquainted with each other and are comfortable working together; (2) students develop their abilities to pretend; (3) students learn to respond to subtle changes in the behavior of other actors in the same situation.[5] The younger the students (grades one through five), the less likely it will be necessary for the teacher to adhere to the stages indicated above. As has been suggested, younger students are generally less inhibited and more eager to use their imaginations than are older students. With students in grade six and beyond, the teacher will find it extremely useful to follow the stages quite carefully.[6]

A Preparatory Sequence

Stage 1. Although it may be difficult to believe, many classrooms exist where students do not know each other's names or are quite unaware of who their classmates really are. It is imperative in role playing that students know each other, not only in terms of names but also in terms of interests, habits, and abilities. To foster this kind of awareness, engage students in a number of exercises such as the following which force them to make contact with each other.

A. To help students learn each other's names, let them play "Name Quickdraw." Tell the students: "Imagine that you are all gunmen out West. Begin walking slowly around the room, making eye contact with other gunmen. As soon as you make eye contact, draw an imaginary gun as quickly as possible and 'shoot' the other person by calling out his name loudly. Whoever calls the other's name correctly first wins the shoot-out and the other person must drop to the floor dead. The gunman who stays up longest wins." (For variation, the losers of each shoot-out can match wits and quickdraws against each other until a champion has been determined in this group as well.)

B. To allow students to get to know more about each

other, divide the class into groups of four to twelve people--the younger the students, the smaller the groups. Have all the group members sit in circles facing each other. Request that one individual in each group begin the game by saying his name and telling the group about something he likes to do, using only a few words: "My name is Ed and I lift weights." "My name is Janie and I make ice cream for fun." Proceeding in a clock-wise direction, the next person repeats what the preceding one has said and then gives his or her name and what he or she likes to do. The process continues until it returns to the starter who must then repeat all the information which has been accumulated. Variations on this game include making the groups smaller and increasing the amount of information to be passed along; pantomiming the information instead of verbalizing it can also be an excellent way to introduce this aspect of dramatization into the open activities. If someone cannot remember a name or detail during the game, others can help by prompting the person. Even classes that have been together for a time enjoy this game because it gives them new opportunities to share information about each other.

C. Another possibility for getting acquainted is to give out interview sheets; these consist of a series of items which must be matched with individuals in a group. Students must move around the room, meeting and talking with each other, until they have completed the sheet by placing a name beside each item. Depending upon the size of the class, the list can be adjusted for the appropriate number of items, thus forcing the student to meet each person in the room at least once. The sheet:

Directions: Locate an individual in the class who fits one of the items below; place that person's name in the appropriate space. Continue until all blanks are filled. Each name may appear only once.

Find a Person Who	Name of Person
1. Has watched five different tv shows in the past two days	________________
2. Plays a non-team sport	________________
3. Has been bike riding lately	________________
4. Thinks that women are equal to men	________________

D. Movement is also important at the beginning stage so students will feel comfortable in the actions of later role plays. The following activities work well for this purpose.

1. Tell the group that they are going to become a huge machine using only their bodies. One person starts the machine by making a repetitive movement such as swinging the arm in a circular fashion. One by one, others join in, attaching themselves to the "starter" and adding their own movements; this should continue until the entire group is interconnected and moving in many different ways. If students are reluctant to begin this activity on their own, place several of the students in motion and then encourage others to join them.
2. A variation on the children's game of Blind Man's Bluff helps many students to relax and become more sensitive to their surroundings and each other. Students should pair off and decide who will be the blind person; this "blind" person is then led by the partner on a tour of the room and parts of the building if possible; the tour should include experiences with various textures--walls, furniture, liquids, clothing--and sounds. As much as possible there should be no physical contact but simply reliance on the other senses and various means of communication devised by the partners; once an individual has had a tour, the roles should be reversed and the other person allowed to have the experience. Group discussion of feelings and problems should occur after the completion of the experience.

Stage 2. Much has been said and written about the need for creativity in schools; too often, however, we have done little to encourage the use of the imagination in the regular classroom setting. For this reason, students find it difficult to suspend their disbelief and let their imaginations take them into unexplored territory just for the thrill of seeing what can be discovered and imagined. Since role playing relies heavily upon the individual's ability to project into another role, it is vital that students experience the process of imagining objects and situations to be something different from what they actually are. Younger children, of course, delight in this kind of activity because it is still a very natural part of their lives; hence, for them, the activities will seem more like games. For the older student, however, activities such as the following will serve as training exercises to regain the ability to pretend and to react imaginatively without being inhibited.

A. Divide the class into several groups if it is quite large or if a fairly small group, keep it together. Hand an object such as a piece of string to each group. Tell the group: "You are each to do something with this object to make it something other than what it presently is and the rest of the group must guess what is being represented. As soon as it is correctly identified, pass the object to the next person on your right who will change the object into something else." Once the groups have performed this activity quite smoothly, change the focus slightly and tell them that instead of the rest of the group's guessing each time, they must now become a part of the object or action being portrayed; for example, if someone was using a piece of rope as a telephone wire, others might perch on it like song birds.

B. Complete group involvement in imaginative activity is important. To help this occur, suggest that students choose up sides and then play a basketball or baseball game in slow motion; after this, have students pair off and play individual sports such as tennis, golf or badminton. No words are to be used during these activities.

C. The more partners students can experience working with, the easier it will be for later role playing where many different roles and relationships will be used. One way of preparing students for this experience is to have them pair off with people they do not know too well and then go through the following sequence. Relying solely on nonverbal communication, they are to act as though meeting for the first time, then discover they have common interests, decide to go somewhere together--dance, movie--and have fun, then become angry, then make up and finally say good-bye. Each of the steps in the sequence should be introduced one at a time as students indicate they are ready for them.

Stage 3. The greatest weakness in role playing is that it may become too mechanical; the teacher establishes a situation and the students go through it obediently, remaining almost totally unaware of the behavior of others in the enactment. If, however, students are aware of the concept of transformation[7] and know how it can be used, they will be more likely to break out of dead-end situations and make them work to their advantage. They can respond to the immediate actions of others in the situation instead of marching single-mindedly in the one direction originally established by the group or the teacher. Being able to make such transformations means the difference between mechanical role playing and organic role development.

The concept of transformation is similar to that of free association; subtle actions or events in a scene become the catalyst for participants to move the scene in new directions. Characters change, settings shift, time passes. This is not capricious activity necessarily but occurs because some sort of association slips into place in an individual's mind. Because effective role playing is the result of spontaneity and because scenes must develop from within rather than entirely from external sources, students need the ability to work together as an organic entity, remaining attuned to the behavior of others in the scene and responding to the subtle shifts that occur in others and in their own awareness.

The following exercises suggest some of the possible ways for training students in the use of transformations. The suggested sequence is intentional since a progression of skills is called for; adaptations for grade levels are easily handled once the basic sequence is understood.[8]

A. Everyone forms a circle; one student begins clapping in a definite rhythm and all the other students pick up and follow the rhythm. Then inform the group that you wish different people to change the rhythm slightly and for everyone else to follow their lead so that all will be using the same rhythm. Let students remain with one rhythm until it is well established; then someone changes the pattern and everyone follows.

B. Once the sense of rhythm has been explored adequately, the notion of interlocking patterns of rhythm should be introduced; here everyone does not need to be doing the same rhythm but the variations must fit together to make an organic whole. Do not let the exercise disintegrate to the point where everyone is doing a different rhythm. Some demonstration may be necessary to aid students in grasping the procedure.

C. To the sound patterns now add movements of the heads and hands so that as the rhythms change, the movements change as well. Again, it may be best to have everyone doing the same movement until they are comfortable and then gradually introduce the variations.

D. Vocal sounds are now substituted for hand-clapping; sounds should be abstract and the variations are worked in as with the hand-clapping. This is followed by having students stand up and add movements besides those of the head and hands to the vocal rhythms. When students appear ready for it, have them substitute abstract body motions for the sounds; the movements should have a rhythm but remain abstract; introduce some variations whenever possible.

E. Gradually introduce purposeful movements to replace the abstract ones. Start students off with a realistic movement such as chopping wood; everyone imitates the pattern of movement until it is well established; then introduce realistic variations.

F. At this point students are ready for longer actions; someone should attempt a realistic action but instead of imitating the action, the group members try to join the action in some way; for example, if someone is trying to direct traffic, some people might become drivers, others pedestrians, still others jay-walkers. After the scene is thoroughly established, someone can introduce a new action and the rest of the group should respond accordingly.

G. The final step in the sequence is for the group to add words to the actions. The greatest difficulty at this point is that students will want to make a play out of the activity. This should not be done. The purpose of the activity is to keep the mind free to respond quickly to whatever is happening. The key principle for students to remember is that if someone is doing something that suggests something else to you, begin doing the thing which you are reminded of.

Once students have become accustomed to the various types of activities outlined above, introduce them to one of the following exercises or a similar one as a measure of their ability to use transformations.

With everyone seated in a circle, have one person give the opening sentence of a story; the person on the right must then add a second sentence; this process continues all the way around the circle until the story is completed. Encourage students to follow the story line rather than attempting to disrupt it.

Place the class in a circle with a volunteer to stand in the center. Another volunteer enters the circle as a particular character; the two people meet and the first person must act appropriately with the second person. After a few minutes, a third person enters the scene and replaces the first person; the third person enters as a new character so the second person must adjust character to suit the situation. This process can continue indefinitely, the scene and characters changing each time a new person enters.

ROLE PLAYING

Getting Ready

Once students have become accustomed to the various aspects of preparing for role playing, they may be introduced to simple role-playing situations. But merely knowing the general problem or idea that students should focus on in role playing is not sufficient to insure success. Too often teachers have misunderstood or failed to plan appropriately for the actual role playing. As a result the participation is limited and everyone becomes discouraged. Role playing may then be labeled as a frivolous device best relegated to the closet where it can languish until some variety is desperately needed for a lesson. Planned and used carefully with students who understand the principles of the activity, however, role playing can become an integral and important part of the learning process.

To begin the role-playing session, be sure that students have had ample opportunity to participate in the sequence of activities just outlined. The next step is called a warm-up and should be used each time role playing occurs. In this stage, students work up to spontaneity and develop their concentration for the experience they will be encountering. Any activities which get the participants moving physically and which help them to remember their relationships with others will be appropriate. Some of the activities suggested in the previous three stages may be used for this purpose.

Once the students have warmed-up, focus their attention on the problem that the role playing will involve. This introduction to the problem or conflict may take a number of forms. If the scene is to involve subject matter being studied, the students can be reminded of this and a quick review of the background leading to the problem will be useful. If the problem will deal with more immediate concerns of the students, they can be asked to consider the problem as it relates to them rather than to the subject matter itself. For instance, the class may have been reading Paul Zindel's novel The Pigman and the students are intrigued by the problem of understanding and relating older people's values and beliefs to their own. To help them make the relationship, the students will role play situations where young people will say or do something which brings them into conflict with an older person's view. The teacher warms the students up for this activity by asking them to talk a bit about older people or relatives they have known; what were some of the differences they noted in the way the older people acted, expressed their views, and related to younger people. After students have discussed these things for a short time, turn their attention to specific situations where they must deal with an older person whose views are contrary to their own.

Introducing the entire group to the problem and allowing them to become familiar with the role-playing focus help to insure that all the students, not just the ones directly playing the roles, will be emotionally drawn into the situation. This involvement means that each person benefits more from identification with the enactment. Whether through direct acting or vicarious experience, each student needs to become a part of the role play.

The Players

Once the warm-up has been concluded, it is time to select the participants. The teacher may choose to describe the characters who will be needed for a scene or the scene may be introduced and students can determine the characters who will be appropriate. Whichever way the selection of players occurs, it should always be done on a voluntary basis. Using volunteers helps to avoid embarrassment and also insures that the people who participate are probably those drawn to the roles. With younger children it is important to involve as many of them as possible, since it is difficult for them to stand by while the action unfolds. For this reason, secondary characters may be placed in the scene to add involvement. Dividing into smaller groups for the purpose of allowing more people to participate is also a good idea, providing students have had prior experience in role playing. If some students are to be an audience, they can be given specific instructions for things to observe and they can be told that they will be the initiators of discussion once the playing ends.

The Playing

After the players have been selected, the scene can be set. Brief instructions are given to the players; depending upon the purpose of the role playing, a specific objective may be given or a more open-ended situation provided. Initially it may be necessary to be quite specific about personal qualities of the various characters, the physical setting, the time and the reactions the characters will have to each other. Every effort, though, should focus on developing the students' abilities to deal with these aspects on their own. Over a period of time, less and less direction should be provided while students accept more and more of the responsibility for developing their own enactments.

For the sake of any audience that may be present and for themselves, the players should briefly describe themselves and the scene, if this has not been done previously. The visualization in the minds of the players and audience provides an important step toward involvement. Furniture, doorways, steps, and other items should be identified while the players move and set their own stage. If difficulties arise, the teacher can ask questions about the time of day, the location of the scene, or the unique features of the room in which the action will take place.

The same kind of activity can be used to present the roles. Each player provides a brief monologue about his character. If the student has difficulty describing the role, the teacher can again resort to the questioning stimulus: "What do you look like?" "How old are you?" "What is your relation to the other characters?"

Once the players have been selected, the scene has been set, and the players have been introduced, the enactment begins. At this point the teacher should withdraw and let the action take over, for as much as possible the players should determine the direction of the scene. Three general guides will help to keep the playing going and can be used as often or as little as necessary.

1. Characters should always be referred to by their role names once they have been selected; this reinforcement helps to keep their attention focused on the roles and encourages them to remain involved in the action.

2. Occasional side coaching of the action may be necessary if an individual drops out of character. Attention should be re-directed to the scene and to the character being played: "I don't believe your wife can hear what you are saying because you are outside the house; where is she?"

3. Scenes often will be short, but no scene should be allowed to drag, and if the focus has been lost, stop the scene quickly. A new scene may be suggested, a new cast assembled, or the group can turn to discussion of the playing.

The Discussion

No role playing should end without a follow-up discussion. Students who become thoroughly involved with their roles need the time to disengage themselves and return to a consideration of what they have experienced. To cut an enactment without discussion may mean that some students will continue in their roles, creating difficulties for themselves and others.

Discussion allows students to reveal insights they may have gained from the playing or viewing of the experience. Since the purpose of role playing often is to show students how they might consider problems in their own lives, discussion provides a forum where these parallels can be explored further without threat or risk. Of special value is audience reaction, for discussion provides a time when they can respond to what they have seen and suggest alternatives. In fact, discussion by role players and the audience usually leads to further enactment, only with new casts. When students know this option is open to them, discussion takes on new dimensions and encourages more response.

Care should be taken during the discussion, however, that none of the players is directly criticized for a portrayal. The teacher avoids this by focusing the discussion on the problem and its relation to students' lives: "How does this problem compare with ones you have encountered in this area?" "How have you handled similar situations in your own life?" When the time comes for re-enactment, students who feel that roles could be played differently can volunteer and provide their interpretations for later discussion. Strong emphasis, though, should be placed on the idea that a role may be played in many different ways; no one way is better than another.

Discussion is a vital aspect of role playing, but it can be of little value unless a proper climate for it has been established previously. Like the preparation for actual role playing, developing an appropriate climate for discussion takes time. One of the best methods for helping students to understand that discussion is not debate or argumentation and that all viewpoints need to be considered is through an adaptation of the guidelines often used for the teaching of values clarification.[9] These guidelines were designed to foster the kind of open discussion that is necessary for an exploration of personal issues. Since role playing frequently assesses and explores various value oriented situations, the teacher should be familiar with the guidelines and their application to role playing.

Any teacher who wishes to use role playing must be accepting and nonjudgmental. Students may be corrected on a factual level, but no right or wrong interpretations of roles actually exist. The teacher may volunteer his own view of the situation, but this is always labeled as an opinion and not offered as a final solution. Avoiding the authoritative tone in responding to role plays will help students respond more honestly in their enactment and follow-up discussions.

Respect for the non-volunteer must be maintained. Not every student is going to be excited about role playing, particularly in the beginning. Such response is natural and should be accepted accordingly. In most cases if emphasis is placed on group involvement as opposed to individual enactment, most students will participate. The gradual development of confidence through preparatory activities and exercises also will encourage the reluctant student. However, at no time should students be forced to participate in an activity which they clearly feel unequal to. Provide alternatives such as becoming part of the audience, serving as a secondary character or becoming a stage manager. The teacher also will want to respect the individual's response. Part of the reward in role playing is the examination of roles and the reaction and evaluation which take place. Questions may be raised about possible solutions to a problem, but the individual's interpretation through role playing should never be directly criticized. In most cases if a role play seems to have missed the point of the problem, reenactment by others will soon rectify the oversight and students will perceive the difference. Handling such problems in this manner will bypass embarrassment for individuals which might, if allowed, discourage them from participating again.

Students who choose to participate in role playing should be encouraged to act honestly. Part of the purpose of role playing is for students to try out new roles, to explore possible ways of behavior, and to feel how someone else feels in a situation. At first it may be very difficult for students to relax and become their roles. If the teacher senses this is a problem, questions can be directed toward the feeling of the role as well as the role behavior: "How do you think the character would feel if this happened?" "How can you describe the feeling inside of you at this moment?" At times role playing calls for the portrayal of stereotypes, but as much as possible, emphasis should go toward creating individualistic roles and responses, drawing upon the players' instincts and feelings as well as knowledge. To detect problems in this area, the teacher must become an expert listener.

Role playing does have limits and they should be observed. Certain roles and certain problem situations may be too controversial or too emotion-laden for some students to handle; pushing into these areas when students exhibit signs of aggression, uneasiness or frustration simply invites difficulties. In some cases a role problem will be beyond the reach of students. They will not have sufficient knowledge or empathy to develop an effective enactment. If this happens, the teacher should quickly stop the action and readjust the focus to a level where success may be assured. Doing this reassures students that they are still operating in a non-threatening environment where the risk-taking is kept to a minimum.

Role playing needs to be tied to adolescent concerns and expectations. Although specific subject matter often will form the core of a role-playing situation, discussion should also relate the enactment to student concerns and social issues whenever possible. The teacher encourages diversity of response and application by occasionally playing the devil's advocate. It sometimes becomes too easy for students to avoid examining all sides of an issue and their own positions in connection with the issue. For role playing to have any lasting effect on attitudes, beliefs, and behavior, it must be reality-centered.

Although no magical way for having good discussion exists, the guidelines above suggest a logical method for establishing a suitable climate in which most students will feel free to respond, to explore, to assess issues which are of concern to them in their everyday lives.

VALUES CLARIFICATION AND ROLE PLAYING

Socialization

Many uses exist for role playing in the classroom and the limits are only those imposed by the imaginations of teachers and students. The teacher needs only to ask whether students will learn more by direct action in dramatization than by discussion alone or whether a concept can become more concrete in the minds of students if they are emotionally and physically involved with it. Grade and ability groupings have little to do with the applicability of role playing.

A frequent use for role playing occurs in those situations where teachers wish to aid students in coming to a better understanding of events and problems that directly touch them in their own lives. At times such concerns may not have a direct bearing on the subject matter being discussed, but because of the nature of the problem or event, discussion and enactment seem both logical and timely. The transfer of a new student into a class, the question of how to treat a person with a handicap, the pending shift in minority populations--these situations can be handled through role playing, providing students with opportunities to test different behaviors and assess their consequences without directly taking a risk in the actual situation. Hypothetical problems can be created to provide the necessary stimulus or other prepared sources may be found.[10]

If at all possible, students should supply the problems which they feel are most pressing. Fannie and George Shaftel suggest the following needs may be the ones that students will wish to address most frequently: a concern about inequalities, an understanding that people are what they are because of their experiences, an awareness of patterns of behavior, an acceptance of duties as citizens, and the knowledge that members of a group are interdependent.[11]

Although emphasis on socialization skills may be more

likely to occur in the elementary school, secondary-school students find this form of role playing just as valuable. For instance, a high-school class might be arguing about the new procedures for recording demerits; a situation can be created quickly and students can provide a number of possible roles. Several enactments could take place in which various points of view, possible alternative plans and solutions are explored. Subsequent discussion should be more reasoned, and comprehension of the entire situation increased. Other possibilities of this type include the following:

A teacher unfairly accuses a student of cheating during an exam.

A teenager comes home two hours after he has told his parents he will be home. They are waiting for him.

A high school student is applying for a summer job during a time when jobs are scarce and he has little experience to offer.

A clerk has overcharged a person and the latter is discussing the matter with him.

A student believes an examination grade is incorrect due to an error on the part of the teacher; they are talking about it.

A very conscientious student who is afraid to do anything irregular has lent term paper notes to a classmate. After the term papers are passed in, the teacher calls the first student into his office and accuses him of plagiarism. How does the student resolve the problem? How does the teacher resolve it?[12]

Clarifying Values

A wide-spread concern exists among adults that many young people do not seem to be living by any consistent set of values. Although it is not unusual in any age to detect a discrepancy between what people say and what people do, modern youth seem to be living their lives without clear purpose and direction, unable to decide what they are for and what they are against.

Dealing with this condition among the students they teach, educators face several choices. They can ignore the problem, hoping it will go away or simply stating that the problem exists but it is one for the home and the church, not the school. A second choice is to transmit an existing set of values to the student, saying that these will "take" and thus solve the problem. A third choice is to help students find their own values. Of the three alternatives, helping students learn the process by which values can be tested and refined seems the most logical, lasting, and beneficial.

But how do we know that students have problems in making value decisions? According to Merrill Harmin and Sidney B. Simon, "A value problem is indicated for a student if, in the absence of prior emotional disturbance, he finds it very difficult to face typical life situations and to make choices and decisions. Or if he typically makes choices without the awareness that some alternatives may be more worthy than others. Or if he does not behave in ways that are consistent with his choices and preferences--that is, if there is a gap between his creeds and his deeds."[13] Another way of saying this is that as young people learn ways of coping with their own crucial life situations, they should be developing the attitudes and values that shape their ways of behaving.

The basic assumption behind teaching values clarification is that humans should arrive at useful values by an intelligent process of choosing, prizing, and behaving.[14] The basic skills in this process are ones which fit easily into role playing situations:

Seeking alternatives when faced with a choice

Looking ahead to probable consequences before choosing

Making choices on one's own, without depending on others

Being aware of one's own preferences and valuations

Being willing to affirm one's choices and preferences publicly

Acting in ways consistent with choices and preferences

Acting in those ways repeatedly with a pattern to one's life.[15]

Values clarification as a teaching method often has had little relationship to the subject matter of the curriculum and research on the effectiveness of various approaches to values is lacking,[16] but values confusion remains in the lives of students. For this reason, teachers should attempt a combination of subject matter, personal concerns, and values skills through role playing as one possible means for dealing with the problem because when a person is required to act "as if" he holds a certain belief, he is more likely to examine the application of that belief to his own life.

Sources for role playing that involve values clarification can come from many places. For example, students can be presented with a problem that encourages them to explore alternative solutions. A situation such as the following could be used for this purpose:

> You are alone and walking home a different way than usual; as you approach a building, you see a man and a woman standing in the doorway. Their conversation is loud and both are quite excited. Suddenly the man pulls the woman's hair, slaps her across the face and then punches her in the mouth. She screams over and over for help.

Using this problem or one like it, ask students to form groups of three. Each person is to tell in turn what action he would take in this situation; one person records the solutions as they are presented. All answers are accepted without judgment or criticism. Once this has been done, invite the groups to come back together and each "secretary" reports the results of each group's discussion. Students then select from the solutions presented those which they would like to try in dramatic form. Several different enactments can occur with discussion following each one. Such activity is an excellent way for showing students that many different methods of solving a problem may be possible and that there are possible solutions to difficulties if we bother to take the time to explore the alternatives.

Another useful activity comes through the use of fantasy. Frequently students will reveal a number of their beliefs and wishes when asked to develop fantasies. Students are asked to write about a fantasy trip they would like to take; guidelines for writing about this trip might include a brief description of where and when their trip takes place; what they see or do on the trip; who goes with them; and what they like best and least about the trip. These written fantasies then serve as the basis for small group enactments followed by discussions where students can explain their choices. This is an effective and safe means for helping students become aware of their values-related feelings and thinking.[17]

For the English teacher who may be concerned that utilizing role playing for values clarification may take the class too far afield from the subject matter being studied, the subject matter itself may be the genesis for effective role playing that leads to concern with values. Literature abounds with a wealth of possibilities for this purpose and such study adds an extra dimension to students' appreciation of what literature has to offer them. For example, Aaron Hillman uses fantasy to introduce students to William Golding's Lord of the Flies. His directions:

> Fantasy: Circle of students. In the middle a table with a rubber mallet. Set the problem: 'You are a group on an airplane flight who have crash-landed on a remote and uncharted island in the vast Pacific. Your pilot is dead; your radio is dead. No one knows you are missing. This group, as you are now, is there. You are alone on the island. It is your problem.' The teacher remains completely silent and assumes the attitude that these students are in that situation. It will take days, but eventually the students will form a government of their own in the same manner as the boys in Lord of the Flies.[18]

Animal stories for younger children present another source for exploration through role playing. In the course of discussing how people and animals seem to share some common characteristics and how we come to associate certain types of people with certain types of animals, students might engage in a value clarifying activity. Tell students they are to select the animal they like best; if they have trouble thinking of animals other than those in the story, list some possibilities on the board. When they have selected their animals, they are to consider three items: (1) what do I like best about this animal--the way it looks, moves, what it represents? (2) how am I most like this animal? (3) how would I like to be more like this animal? Students may then role play their animals for others. This activity often provides students, particularly younger ones, with an opportunity to affirm a behavior pattern they find attractive or to attempt some behavior that is completely different for them but which they think they might like to adopt; for instance, the shy student who might like to become a tiger in order to be more aggressive.

A strategy that can be used successfully with almost any piece of literature is that called the "strength whip" or "proud whim." The purpose of the activity is to get students to accentuate the positive aspects in their lives. Initially, it might be introduced through a novel such as John Steinbeck's The Pearl. Depending on the size of the class, have students form a circle or several small circles. Ask the group members to imagine that they are the chief character in the novel, Kino. Focusing on a specific chapter or series of chapters in the book, each student as Kino is to present one item that he is proud of; each person will be called on in rapid succession until all have had an opportunity to share their thoughts. Students may pass a turn if they choose but they should try to enter into subsequent rounds.

Some possible responses for this whip might include the following statements, based on chapter four of the novel: "I was strong in my demands when selling the pearl." "I did not lose my temper when intimidated." "I did not accept a sum which I didn't believe to be fair." "I fought to protect my possessions."[19]

From this point students might later be encouraged to produce their own proud whips during which they offer things which they feel proud of about themselves. After such experiences, students should have ample opportunity to discuss and explain why these items are positive aspects of their character.

Using various forms of literature as a basis, students can establish interview situations with characters. The class interviews the character as played by a classmate and this individual must answer as he feels the character would. For example, some student might play the role of the doctor in The Pearl. The class could ask questions about the doctor's feelings and reactions when Kino came to him the first time. After the interview has been completed, students might then examine their own feelings and reactions in this situation and discuss them with each other.

Literature, then, provides a rich resource for all kinds of role playing, whether it is values oriented or not. Teachers at all levels should have no difficulty finding and using literary sources that will encourage students to examine not only the events and characters within the works but also the relationship of these things to their own day-to-day living. In this way, values clarification easily can be related to subject matter.

Role Taking

One important distinction should be made about the essential difference between role taking and role playing, since the terms are often used interchangeably. In role taking the focus is upon taking roles and responding to them as though the players themselves were in the situations. In role playing, people take the parts of others but try to act and respond as they imagine these individuals would. For example, in a role taking situation, the individual might be asked: "If you were the parent of a seventeen-year-old-girl, how would you react when informed by the local police that she had been booked on a driving-while-intoxicated charge?" In contrast, consider the role-play situation where a student becomes the Hobbit of J. R. R. Tolkien's The Lord of the Rings trilogy and has to explain why he chose to do some of the things he did. Here the student must assume the philosophy and actions of the character, thus removing the role play from being centered immediately on reality. Because of this distinction, role taking tends to work best in values clarification situations where the emphasis is most apt to be on the student's own life and problems.

Role Playing in Perspective

Role playing is not a new technique nor is it the answer to all our problems in the classroom. What it does provide is a flexibility often lacking in other modes of instruction such as the lecture, the group discussion, the oral report. Teachers should not see their roles in the classroom as ones of putting things into the minds of children without provision for other means of learning. Why shouldn't a child be permitted to learn other ways of coping with his own crucial life situations. As Maurice P. Hunt and Lawrence Metcalf point out, "The critical test of a person's insights is whether they provide him with a set of beliefs about himself in relation to his social and physical environment which are extensive in scope, dependable in action, and compatible with one another."[20]

Through role playing, with the guidance of skillful and perceptive teachers who thoroughly understand and believe in the value of the process, children and adolescents can develop heightened sensitivity to the human consequences of the choices they make in their everyday lives. This will only happen, however, if students are given the necessary freedom to respond in creative ways and to allow their enactments to evolve organically rather than as merely another mechanical task. It is to this end that all role playing should be directed.

References

[1]See Gene Stanford, "Why Role Playing Fails," English Journal 63 (December 1974), 50-54.

[2]Role-playing for Social Values (Englewood Cliffs, N.J.: Prentice-Hall, 1967), p. 9.

[3]Ibid., pp. 9-10.

[4]Gene Stanford and Albert E. Roark, Human Interaction in Education (Boston: Allyn and Bacon, 1974), pp. 173-174.

[5]Ibid., p. 178.

[6]Some of the activities in this sequence are adapted from Stanford and Roark, pp. 179-186.

[7]Stanford and Roark, p. 186.

[8]Adapted from Stanford and Roark, pp. 187-190.

[9]Merrill Harmin et al., Clarifying Values through Subject Matter (Minneapolis: Winston Press, 1973), pp. 37-38.

[10]See Shaftels' Role-playing for Social Values (reference 2), which contains a number of excellent stories for this purpose.

[11]Role Playing the Problem Story (New York: Commission on Educational Organization, National Conference of Christians and Jews, 1952), p. 48.

[12]Charles R. Duke, Creative Dramatics and English Teaching (Urbana, Ill.: NCTE, 1974), p. 104.

[13]"Values," in Readings in Values Clarification, eds. Merrill Harmin and Sidney B. Simon (Minneapolis: Winston Press, 1973), p. 5.

[14]Elementary teachers will find "A Strategy for Teaching Values," a filmstrip/cassette kit (Guidance Associates, Pleasantville, N.Y., 1972) an excellent in-service program for becoming familiar with the values process; secondary teachers may find Sidney Simon's "Values in Teaching," a speech made at the 1971 Ohio Catholic Education Association Convention, a helpful introduction (available on cassette from Creative Sights and Sounds, Inc., 2453 East River Road, Dayton, Ohio). Also useful for all levels as the chief philosophical statement on values clarification is Louis E. Raths et al., Values and Teaching (Columbus, Ohio: Charles E. Merrill, 1966).

[15]"Values," in Reading in Values Clarification, pp. 13-14.

[16]See Howard Kirschenbaum's "Beyond Values Clarification," in Readings in Values Clarification, pp. 92-110, for some provocative thoughts about future directions for this type of teaching.

[17]Adapted from Leland W. Howe and Mary Martha Howe, Personalizing Education, Values Clarification and Beyond (New York: Hart Pub. Co., 1975).

[18]As cited in George Isaac Brown, Human Teaching for Human Learning; An Introduction to Confluent Education (New York: Viking Press, 1971), pp. 62-63.

[19]Adapted from Howe and Howe, p. 426.

[20]Teaching High School Social Studies (New York: Harper and Row, 1955), p. 52.

EDUCATIONAL DRAMA AND LANGUAGE DEVELOPMENT

Betty Jane Wagner

Educational drama or creative dramatics encompasses all dramatic activities that are largely improvisational and created by the participants themselves. These include spontaneous drama with its tension and conflict, warm-up movements, pantomime, acting-out games, puppet shows, dramatic play, and other unrehearsed expressions in gesture, words, and action in the context of an imagined situation. How do such varied activities as these help students develop language?

Obviously, educational drama does not develop language by leading students to the mastery of a script. Participants in educational drama typically do not begin with a text as actors do. Even if they do an improvisation that takes off from a story or poem, they work out the interaction of the characters with spontaneous, not memorized, dialogue and actions. Their material for the drama may come from literature, but they add to it their own experience or their inner fantasy. Because participants make up the details as they go along, not only are they pressed to produce language, but they capture the vitality and tension of spontaneous human interaction as well. None of them is quite sure where the drama will lead. Drama as a process provides a natural way to use language and a way to capture "the primitive element of group participation in a here-and-now event. Because there is minimal delay of response or abstracting and categorizing, the experience is close to the natural mode of both the young child and the openly involved adult."[1]

Educational drama is valuable in many ways, such as in providing a way for a participant to build social skills or to work through urgent personal problems or psychic tensions; but here we shall consider only those ways that drama can develop competence in the language arts of speaking, listening, and by extension, writing as well. The goal in all language education is the development of the ability to send and receive increasingly complex and mature verbal messages effectively, independently, creatively, and symbolically. Educational drama is particularly well suited to facilitate the achievement of this overall goal.

The recognition that educational drama is an effective way to develop a child's oral language goes back at least a hundred years. In the 1880's, Francis W. Parker, as head of the Department of Didactics at Martha's Vineyard Summer Institute, was lecturing to urge the use of simple improvised activities as an excellent technique for the development of oral expression.

Improvising or inventing, whether through classroom drama or on one's own, is at the heart of all oral language development. No toddler ever matures as a speaker until he makes up sentences he has never heard before. He or she plays with options, tries out new forms, and makes up his own utterances by putting together in a novel way the language he has heard. Educational drama provides a stimulus for the continuation of this valuable activity.

Building Vocabulary

The most obvious way that drama enlarges a child's fund of words is by providing a natural need for using words that are already in his passive vocabulary. If he is acting out a story he has heard, he gradually gains control over words that may be only fuzzily familiar. For example, once he is actively addressing the wicked, ugly troll, as in a story the teacher may have just told or read to the class, that phrase may be assertively affirmed, "You are mean and you are bad; I hate you, you wicked, ugly troll!" The act of utterance makes the phrase his own.

Often a teacher in role as one of the characters in the drama can feed into the interaction new or more precise vocabulary in such a way that it is unobtrusive but helpful. For example, if one of the children is a Queen, the teacher can address her as "Your Royal Highness" and bid the others to enter into her royal presence. As the teacher thus lifts the language, she not only gives dignity to the performance but feeds in apt vocabulary.

Several significant research studies have shown that groups of children who have had regular creative dramatics experiences in the classroom have made greater gains in language arts, including the mastery of a larger vocabulary and reading skill, than control groups who have not had drama.[2] In one program called Improvise, five drama teachers toured the state of Rhode Island teaching creative dramatics to groups of fourth graders in a 15-week experiment. At the end of the period the groups that had had drama showed a vocabulary growth double that of a control group.[3]

One elementary teacher, Silvia Diane Bordan, had her third-graders keep a personal dictionary listing in alphabetical order all the new words they had found useful in classroom drama. Beside each word they put the definition they had discussed in class after each drama session was over, or, in the case of the more mature children, the definition they looked up in the dictionary. Then each child wrote a sentence the teacher dictated using the new vocabulary word and underneath that he wrote a sentence of his own. At the end of the year most of her third graders had improved two years in vocabulary and a year and a half in reading as measured by standardized tests.[4]

Not only does drama introduce new words and more words from the child's passive to his active vocabulary, but it also sharpens the edges of the words he already uses. One can learn the effect of his words only by trying them out on others. Rhetorical style is honed on the whetstone of response. Both actual conversation and improvised drama provide this response and pressure for reshaping an utterance to achieve the desired effect. For example, if in a drama a child knocks on a door and says weakly, "Let me in," and nothing happens, and he repeats this several times with the same result, he may finally be moved to a majestic, "Open this door in the name of the King!" He has felt a pressure to change his diction and to project his words with determination and vigor.

Moving Away from Egocentricity

In the process of sharpening his vocabulary, a drama participant learns to adapt his communication to his situation and to the needs of his listeners. In other words, he engages in the art of rhetoric. Educational drama performs a valuable service in helping a child overcome his immature egocentricity. This is the term Jean Piaget used in his classic study of the language development of children in which he identified two distinct stages: egocentric language that is uttered by a child to no particular person and for no particular purpose, and adapted communication that is socialized. A child adapts his communication to influence another specific person; in order to be successful he must take into account the point of view of the other.[5]

As long as a child's language is egocentric, it is considered deficient, at least in a larger public than his own home. He is unable to create meaning within another individual.[6] What the child says simply cannot be translated into a message. The most common reason a child cannot create meaning for his listener is not that he stutters or speaks in garbled phrases, or slurs his words or even uses incorrect English, but, rather, that he fails to take account of the other as other. He seems to assume the listener can read his mind. In the case of the young child, his parents indeed may seem to read his mind for they often become adept at interpreting the toddler's private egocentric speech since they have been listening to it as the child has babbled along in accompaniment to his actions. His or her own private and idocyncratic language is shared with them. However, as the child's social groups widens, he finds he must use language according to the conventions of a larger public, must adapt his communication to another person, or he will be misunderstood. For example, a child might find the word "bambaw" gets him a banana in intimate interaction with his parents, but when he is at Grandma's he has to say, "want banana"--a sentence he discovers he can generate but has never yet needed to use.

The single, most plaguing deterrent to effective communication, orally or in writing, for both children and adults, is the fact of egocentricity or the failure to take into account what one's words must mean to others. The problem comes to the surface most often in children's written compositions, for there no accompanying gesture or intonation pattern helps his reader decipher the message. On the other hand, a student who has learned to communicate well has had to transcend his egocentricity; he or she has had to role play the intended receiver of his message well enough to spell out private or ambiguous references and to be aware that his reader's experience, attitude, or values may well differ from his own. Effective communication calls for decentering, rising above one's egocentricity and putting oneself into the role of the listener. Several significant research studies have shown that creative dramatics experience increases a child's capacity to put himself into the role of another person and thereby adapt his communication with that other person.[7]

Drama is invented conversation--dialogue that mirrors the interactions of real life. True dialogue is never a simple transfer of what is inside one person's being to the head or heart of another. It is useful to remember Martin Buber's conception of the primordial "I-Thou" relationship which defines dialogue as address and response and the reality of meeting and of the "between." It is all of this that drama captures. The word that moves between human beings in an actual or invented dialogue moves in tension, for two persons almost never mean exactly the same thing by the words they use. Each brings to the conversation a different set of experiences and feelings; no response to one's words is ever fully satisfactory. There is always more to explore, for "at each point of the dialogue, understanding and misunderstanding are interwoven. From this tension of understanding and misunderstanding comes the interplay of openness and closeness, expression and reserve that mark every genuine dialogue."[8]

The goal of all education is to enable students to mature to the point where they can engage in this genuine dialogue. Michael Oakeschott even went so far as to say that our whole culture is nothing but an extended dialogue "a conversation, begun in the primeval forests and made more articulate in the course of centuries."[9] Surely undoing egocentricity to the point where one can converse not only with those persons of his own time but with those of ages past as well is a worthy educational goal and one to which educational drama makes a significant contribution.

Developing Fluency

Because educational drama calls forth speech in a natural, life-like situation, it builds self-confidence in speakers. As children discover that they can move and speak appropriately in a wide variety of situations, they have a solid, successful experience to build on in their actual real-life interactions. Each imagined situation in drama is different; through responding aptly to each challenge, children gain an intuitive understanding of various styles of response. They try out different voices, stances and rhetorical ploys.

As a child experiences a wide variety of roles, he gains insight into the many opinions, attitudes and evaluations that characterize the individuals in our society. These varied voices often contradict one another in ways that not even a sage could resolve. Maturity consists in learning to tolerate these myriad voices not only in the community in which one lives but also in oneself, for the dialogue one participates in becomes internalized in oneself. As Douglas Barnes put it, "Each must learn to tolerate the many voices within himself, to recognize and express his own variousness, to learn how to live amongst uncertainties and divided loyalties."[10] Thinking, and ultimately essay-writing skill, is rooted in active inner dialogue and an imaginative role-playing of the intended listener or reader in order to anticipate his questions and possible confusions and to deal with them. One learns to speak and write convincingly to the degree that one internalizes the various dialogues he or she has heard and incorporates them in his or her own thinking and, ultimately, monologues--oral and written.

Because our society is complex and its voices many, we need to educate children to be able to choose and to assume responsibility for their choices--to act on them. One way to do this is to help them actively explore society's many voices through drama.

Drama demands not only choice, but fluency--the ability to move quickly from one challenge or idea to another. In any situation there are many possibilities or responses, but there is also a pressure for choice among alternatives. This creates a tension through which children learn to respond aptly and with dispatch to the demands of the moment. In order to be able to respond quickly, they must listen with care to what others are saying and watch their actions closely.

Participants in a drama find they need to develop a wider range of dialects. The pressure of assuming a role is one of the most effective stimuli for a child who speaks a nonstandard dialect to practice standard dialect.

No matter what the dialect, however, a child participating in drama faces pressure from his peers to articulate the sounds of speech clearly. One of the many research studies that show that classroom drama increases a child's power over language was that of Barbara McIntyre, who, in a controlled experiment with students with speech disorders, showed that the experimental group that participated in creative dramatics made a significant reduction in the number of consonant articulation errors.[11] In a study by E. Irwin of emotionally disturbed boys, the experimental group which had creative drama showed significantly greater improvement on verbal fluency tests than did the groups who were treated with activity, psychotherapy, and recreation respectively.[12]

It is no surprise that articulation and fluency should improve with drama. Children have to speak so they can be heard and understood if they are to get on with the drama, and they are constantly having to adapt their thinking to the suggestions and direction of other individuals. The outcome of what they have begun together is always unpredictable, so they need to make discoveries together. For example, if the students as pirates uncover an ornate cask deep in the ground, they might all gather around while the teacher holds back the action. "Wait until we can all see before you open it. It seems to be locked. What shall we do without a key?" etc. When the children finally do get the chest open, whatever the first child who shares his vision says he sees will have to be accepted by the rest of the group. If one child decides it is empty, the rest will have to get all their own images of diamonds and jewels out of their heads and focus on the disappointment of an empty chest. This calls for agility in response and is a powerful stimulus for the development of creative thinking.

Another thing that responding to an imagined situation does is make the participants sensitive, as they go through the motions of an imagined action, to the particularity of sense experiences they remember. Even the simplest everyday task is made up of a number of separate actions and sensory experiences which when remembered become a source of insight. Verbal fluency for the child often flows more freely in the presence of actual or imagined objects or actions. Children who become better observers and participants in real life strengthen their sensibility both in real life and in drama; fully realized concrete experiences provide the basis for both dramatic enactments and for the development of more abstract thought at a later stage. In addition, most concrete experiences are fused with emotion which gives them power, which in turn energizes speech.

Improving Discussion Skills

Drama is best considered as a regular part of all the talk that regularly goes on in an elementary classroom. When engaged in a group task, the talk is task-centered; when focused on an idea, it is topic-centered. Planning for, enacting, and evaluating a classroom drama calls forth both kinds of discussion. The process of deciding how to dramatize a certain situation, where the first scene should be, who should play which part--all is task talk. While a scene is being enacted, the characters in the drama may find themselves engaging in a group task, and accompanying this will be lively task talk. From time to time, still within the dramatic situation, the various characters may need to hold a conference--a discussion on broader topics than those that focus on task, such as, What is the most important thing for our tribe to teach its children? What would happen if we just cooperated in sharing this land and didn't fence it off into separate pieces for each family? Do we need to have a school in this place? or Is there a better way to govern our village?

Topic-centered discussion appropriately follows a classroom drama. Participants and observers make evaluations of the effectiveness of the scene and suggestions for improving the performance the next time. For example, if a child needs to sharpen his articulation, his peers will usually know it, and their prodding, "I couldn't understand what you said" is usually more effective than teacher-led exercises in pronunciation. Sometimes a teacher stops a drama that is not going well and asks the class to figure a way out of their impasse. At other times she pushes them for a reflection on the universal meaning of a particular enactment. The side effect of this focused discussion is the acceleration of language learning. Like dramatic inventing, task and topic talk are social activities; all three build toward skill in listening and apt response.

Conclusion

In 1957, Winifred Ward noted that creative dramatics was then viewed in four widely different ways: as a tool to involve children in learning facts, as pure recreation, as therapy, and "as an art with such unquestioned value that it should be a part of every elementary school curriculum, on equal footing with music and graphic and plastic arts."[13]

It was only this last view that Winifred Ward espoused; but, as Geraldine Brain Siks pointed out, the sad fact is that we are still far from the day when the fourth attitude, and with it the inclusion of creative dramatics as a basic part of all elementary-school curricula, is a reality. Drama should never be viewed as just a way to sugar-coat facts; they may be learned in other and often more efficient ways. Recreation and therapy, although desirable, are not the primary function of the school.

Fortunately, however, until such time as drama as an art, and indeed the graphic and plastic arts and music and dance as well, are considered the basic and not a peripheral curriculum for young children--the expressive matrix out of which all cognitive learning develops--we can make a persuasive case for drama by showing its effect on oral language, and at one remove on reading and writing as well. In so doing we assert that drama is nothing less than the "basic skill" that is the foundation of all language development.

References

[1]James Moffett and Betty Jane Wagner, Student-Centered Language Arts and Reading, K-13 (Boston: Houghton Mifflin Co., 1976), p. 85.

[2]One such study was that of William Earl Blank, "The Effectiveness of Creative Dramatics in Developing Voice, Vocabulary and Personality in the Primary Grades," Ph.D. dissertation, University of Denver, 1953.

[3]"Creative Dramatics Spurs Verbal Development in Rhode Island," Nation's Schools 90 (September 1972), 51-52.

[4]Sylvia Diane Bordan, Plays as Teaching Tools in the Elementary School (West Nyack, N.Y.: Parker Pub. Co., 1970).

[5]Jean Piaget, The Language and Thought of the Child (London: Routledge and Kegan Paul, 1926), p. 34.

[6]D.C. Barnlund, "Toward a Meaning-Centered Philosophy of Communication," Journal of Communication 12 (1963), 197-211.

[7]See, for example, Mary E. Lunz, "The Effects of Overt Dramatic Enactment on Communication Effectiveness and Role Taking Ability," Ph.D. dissertation, Northwestern University, 1974.

[8]Maurice Friedman, introductory essay to Martin Buber and the Theater, ed. and transl. by Maurice Friedman (New York: Funk and Wagnalls, 1969).

[9]Michael Oakeshott, essay in R. R. Peters' symposium, The Concept of Education (London: Routledge & Kegan Paul, 1967).

[10]Douglas Barnes, ed., Drama in the English Classroom (Champaign, Ill.: National Council of Teachers of English, 1968), p. 2.

[11]Barbara M. McIntyre, "The Effect of a Program of Creative Activities upon the Consonant Articulation Skills of Adolescent and Pre-Adolescent Children with Speech Disorders," Ph.D. dissertation, University of Pittsburgh, 1957.

[12]E. Irwin, "The Effects of a Program of Creative Dramatics Upon Personality as Measured by the California Test of Personality, Sociograms, Teacher Ratings, and Grades," Ph.D. dissertation, University of Pittsburgh, 1963.

[13]Winifred Ward, Playmaking with Children, (New York: D. Appleton-Century, 1957), p. 16.

EDUCATIONAL DRAMA AND MORAL DEVELOPMENT

Denny T. Wolfe, Jr.

Historically, during times of great societal stress, people have turned to the schools in hopes of simultaneously finding causes of the disturbance and solutions for restoring calm. Such is the case today. In recent years, for example, juvenile crime has advanced at a terrifically accelerated pace. Many citizens are accusing schools for failing to hold students until graduation and failing to prepare them adequately for responsible citizenship. Ironically, educators always seem to be cast into roles of both scapegoats and heroes. This is to say, when things go wrong--when "the center cannot hold," as Yeats expressed it--people blame the schools; however, schools are also expected to solve problems that other institutions admittedly cannot.

In the fifties, after the Russians forged ahead in the "moon marathon," Americans pointed reproachfully at the schools for failing to produce students with adequate backgrounds in science learning. As a response to this apparent failing, the National Defense Education Act of 1958 created an unprecedented flow of federal dollars into the schools, directed toward the improvement of teaching and learning in the areas of science, math, and modern languages. More and more, however, educators are beginning to see that <u>quantitative</u> responses to problems in the schools are not adequate for producing <u>qualitative</u> change. Such responses are necessary, but they are not, in themselves, sufficient. Qualitative responses--or, how can we find <u>different</u> ways to produce <u>better</u> results?--must be found to improve schooling in significant ways.

Turning to the history of English education, a landmark event in the search for qualitative change was the Anglo-American Seminar on the Teaching of English (1966), held on the campus of Dartmouth College and aimed toward strengthening the curriculum in language and literature. Perhaps the most important contribution of the British at that conference was their advocacy of a student-centered curriculum, meant to humanize the educational process. Since then, helping students achieve "personal growth" has been a major goal of English teaching.

For English educators today, the desire to create "the great personalized curriculum" has taken its place alongside the desire to write "the great American novel" as an ideal toward which to strive. And the frustrations of realizing such idealistic goals are also quite the same. How would we recognize either if we saw it? Yet, certainly, we must continue to try--if not to write the improbable "great American novel"--at least to humanize the curriculum in schools so that students will learn to live productively, happily, and peacefully in what has become a global society.

At present, however, American education is passing through another "Back to Basics" phase. There is, of course, nothing wrong with such a phase, provided the view is <u>future</u>-focused. In the wake of Watergate, it would appear that nothing is more basic for Americans today than capturing a strong sense of self-respect and moral behavior, both as a nation and as separate individuals. Helping students achieve literacy is an unquestionably "basic" goal for schools, but it is significant to note that Adolph Hitler rose to power in one of the most literate nations of the world.

Educational literature and current reports from the mass media are filled with evidence that schools are not very delightful places to be, neither for students nor for teachers nor for administrators. This phenomenon is not at all new, but it has hardly been more prolifically nor more vividly documented than it has recently. Teachers threaten students; students threaten teachers; and sometimes the threats turn into actual violence. Everyone who has worked in schools lately has stories to tell which appall and even outrage the uninitiated. A crucial issue for modern education is whether or not schools can operate in a spirit of mutual cooperation among those who pay for them, those who run them, and those who attend them. If a favorable resolution to this issue is to occur, one thing that must be done is to place major emphasis in schools upon teaching for moral development. In the final analysis, students can become considerate, humane, stable, and independently-thinking adults only if they are stimulated to aspire toward progressively higher stages of moral reasoning.

WHAT IS MORAL DEVELOPMENT?

"Development" suggests that something already exists upon which one can continue to build. If we are to speak of creating a brand new thing, we must use a word other than "development." By using the phrase "moral development," therefore, we are assuming that by the time a student steps into our classrooms, he/she is bringing at least some rudimentary elements of a moral foundation which has already been established and which can be further developed. That is to say, the student has had to make decisions based upon his/her perceptions of right and wrong. Rightness and wrongness, as I use the terms here, have to do with morality and not necessarily with religion. To draw a distinction, I suggest that religion has to do with the relationship between a person and his/her God; morality has to do with the relationship between one person and another, and also between two nebulous entities which I will call mind and conscience. One could call them self and soul, but those terms are even less precise than the ones I have selected: Mind = logically reasoning intellect; Conscience = innate and intuitive sense of right (that which feels good to the psyche) and wrong (that which the psyche rejects). The problem here, then, is to discover ways to refine the sensitivity of the psyche so that it becomes increasingly more discriminating about what makes it feel "good" and what makes it feel "bad." This issue lies at the heart of teaching for moral development.

One cannot spontaneously become a sophisticated moral decision-maker. Moral decision-making is a "basic" developmental skill; therefore, classroom strategies must be carefully designed to give students practice in cultivating this skill. That is, students must be given opportunities to choose and to function as independent learners and moral decision-makers. Too many classroom environments are structured in such a way that students are seldom, if ever, given such opportunities. Wilson Riles, Superintendent of Schools for the state of California, describes the situation as follows: "We cannot expect a student to function as a responsible 'choosing, prizing, and acting' citizen at age 18 when his sole knowledge of rights, responsibilities, freedom, justice, and brotherhood has come from negative experiences--from punishment for breaking rules he had no voice in making, from school courses and future occupations chosen for him, from uneven justice for antisocial behavior, from teachers' or administrators' ridicule of individuals, and from too frequent evidence that 'good' guys finish last."[1] If schools are to teach for moral development, the message which must be transmitted to students is that high-level moral behavior is valuable and rewarding. To transmit such a message successfully, not only must teachers' and administrators' attitudes toward students change, but the ways in which moral development occurs in people must be better understood.

The Concept of 'Stages': Freud and Piaget

Administrators, teachers, parents, and students alike can be aided in developing mutual tolerance, respect, and understanding by acting on the knowledge that people pass through various stages of growth. Discovering the stages of a particular student's development can enable parents and educators to arrive at realistic expectations of that student's performance and overall behavior. Developing such realistic expectations permits parents, teachers, and administrators to deal with students in ways that will increase the frequency of success and decrease the frequency of frustration for all concerned.

Sigmund Freud[2] observed that very young children pass through a series of stages in their physical and psychological growth: (1) the *oral stage*, characterized by a baby's sucking as a source of pleasure; (2) the *anal stage*, characterized by deriving pleasure from the moment of internal organs such as the bowels; and (3) the *phallic stage*, characterized by pleasure derived from feelings in sexual organs. Freud believed that these stages influence much of what an individual becomes in later life. It is important to note Freud's observations, only to underscore the idea that much of what students are when they enter our classrooms has been established some time ago. Teachers must become actively aware of this fact because it is crucial to an understanding of "who students are." All students are operating at differing stages of development, and knowing where a student is and has been in the developmental process is necessary to designing successful instructional plans.

A student is a composite of experiences, some common and some uncommon to his/her peers. This recognition is a significant factor in accounting for individual differences and creating an experience-based curriculum. What are the experiences that students share in common? What are the uncommon experiences that are particular to certain individuals? These are questions which teachers must constantly be attempting to answer and to capitalize upon in their efforts to humanize the classroom environment and to facilitate students' growth.

The student is an organic whole, and he/she must be dealt with all at once. An important implication here is that the practice of isolating bits and pieces of knowledge to be taught, learned, and "checked off" does violence to the concept of the holistic quality of both teachers and students. Cognitive and personal growth learning must occur simultaneously if the educational enterprise is to work well. Moral education cannot be taught in a vacuum, nor can it be taught overtly. It must be connected to authentic experiences within the psychological and cultural context of the whole person.

Following Freud's stage model, Jean Piaget sought to discover the thought processes of children.[3] He concluded that people develop their powers of logical thinking in a particular sequence, and, for Piaget, it is not possible to skip stages: (1) the sensorimotor stage is characterized by the use of physical senses to learn about one's life space, and it ends with the beginning of language learning at about age two; (2) the preoperational stage is characterized by rapid language and thought development, egocentricity, and difficulty in distinguishing between real and imaginary experience (this stage ends at approximately age seven in a normally developing child); (3) the concrete operational stage, typically lasting to about age 11, is characterized by logical handling of concrete problems, such as counting, classifying, remembering (however, in this stage, one cannot do abstract thinking); and (4) the formal operational stage, to about age 15, represents full maturation of the cognitive processes, in which one learns to think abstractly and to formulate theories and hypotheses. Some people never reach this stage, a fact which has obvious implications for teaching. Blithely requiring students who have not reached stage 4 to do abstract thinking leads only to total frustration.

The Stages of Moral Reasoning

Lawrence Kohlberg and Elliot Turiel employ the concept of stages to deal specifically with moral development.[4] They believe that teachers should look upon students as "moral philosophers."[5] Further, a teacher must assume the posture of both a "moral philosopher" and a "moral psychologist" in order to understand and to stimulate students' growth. That is not to say, however, that the teacher's task is simply to inculcate a collection of moral values; neither is it to say that the teacher should adopt an "anything goes" posture, whereby students' moral reasoning is, with a wave of the hand, unconditionally accepted as it is. The teacher as moral philosopher and moral psychologist must discover a student's particular stage of development, arouse in the student real moral conflicts about real problems, and present modes of thought one stage above the diagnosed stage of the student.[6] By such a process, the teacher stimulates moral development.

Based upon years of research and experimentation, Kohlberg and Turiel have reported "seven culturally universal stages of moral development" as follows:

I. Stage O: Premoral Stage

One neither understands rules nor judges good or bad in terms of rules and authority. Good is what is pleasing or exciting; bad is what is painful or fearful.

II. Preconventional Level

One is responsive to cultural rules and labels of good and bad, right or wrong, but interprets these labels in terms of either the physical or the hedonistic consequences of action (punishment, reward, exchange of favors) or in terms of the physical power of those who enunciate the rules and labels.

Stage #1: The physical consequences (pain) of action determine its goodness or badness; one values the avoidance of pain.

Stage #2: Right action consists of that which satisfies (rewards) one's own needs and occasionally the needs of others. 'You scratch my back and I'll scratch yours.'

III. Conventional Level

Maintaining the expectations of one's family,

group, or nation is perceived as valuable in its own right. The attitude is one of conformity, loyalty, support, and justification of the existing social order.

Stage # 3: Good behavior is that which pleases or helps others and is approved by them. One earns approval by being 'nice.'

Stage # 4: This is the 'law and order' orientation, characterized by 'doing one's duty,' respecting authority and maintaining the social order for its own sake.

IV. Post Conventional, Autonomous, or Principled Level

One defines moral values and principles which have validity and application apart from the authority of the groups or persons holding these principles and apart from the individual's own identification with these groups.

Stage # 5: This is the social-contract legalistic orientation. Right action is defined in terms of standards which have been critically examined and agreed upon by the whole society. The result is an emphasis upon the legal point of view, but with an emphasis upon the possibility of changing law in terms of rational consideration of social utility. Outside the legal realm, free agreement and contract is the binding element of obligation. This is the 'official' morality of the American government and Constitution.

Stage # 6: This is the universal ethical principle orientation. Right is defined by the decision of conscience in accord with self-chosen ethical principles appealing to logical comprehensiveness, universality, and consistency. These principles are abstract and ethical. At heart, these are universal principles of justice, of the reciprocity and equality of the human rights, and of respect for the dignity of human beings as individuals.[7]

These stages occur developmentally and cannot be skipped. Together with strategies taken from educational drama, they can inform effective methods of teaching for moral development.

EDUCATIONAL DRAMA FOR MORAL DEVELOPMENT

The value of educational drama for use in English teaching has been well supported in recent literature. James Moffett defines drama as "any raw phenomena as they are first being converted to information by some observer."[8] Such conversion is made possible through fresh experiences in life. If we accept a succession of experiences as one definition of living, then the scope of drama goes beyond mere imitation. Drama and real life become synonymous. Moffett, therefore, argues that drama should be central to the English curriculum.

Stephen Judy, citing the expanding roles that people assume through life, notes that drama is "intimately connected with personal growth and development."[9] Any relationship between and among people has a dramatic quality, obviously. And, through the process of group-to-group or one-to-one interaction, people influence one another and pass through stages of growth at varying rates. It is possible for the teacher, by providing high-quality experiences for students in the classroom, to stimulate and to accelerate both cognitive and personal growth. Such experiences must challenge students significantly, however. Dull, seemingly meaningless, and "easy" interaction will not stimulate growth; indeed, it may well retard growth. For schools to influence the developmental processes of students, therefore, classroom environments must often be noisy and dynamic rather than still and passive. Educational drama can create dynamic learning environments if it provides tense situations which require students to struggle and to stretch themselves toward increasingly higher levels of growth.

The Concept of Tension

In her film Three Looms Waiting, Dorothy Heathcote declares that drama is "a real man in a mess." And in a speech delivered in Raleigh, North Carolina, in June 1975, Mrs. Heathcote, discussing the process of education, declared, "If the teacher puts the tension there, the rest will follow." Certainly, creating healthy learning tension in the classroom is a delicate matter. As noted earlier, if a student has not yet reached Piaget's level of formal operations, and is required to do abstract thinking, then the student is doomed to failure. If a student is operating at Kohlberg's and Turiel's stage 2 moral reasoning, and is being pushed toward stage 4 or higher, then the tension created invariably is going to be unhealthy. Students can be stimulated to grow only one stage at a time, i.e., stages cannot be skipped, according to the bulk of research on personal development. But tension that requires students to perform tasks which they can realistically be expected to perform has a positive learning value. In fact, moral development--like drama--requires the element of tension.

Jane Loeinger, professor of psychology at Washington University, claims that "simultaneously holding in mind opposite ideas or opposing solutions to a problem, may be one way of achieving moral or ego growth."[10] She further declares that "a clash of moral opinions"[11] may be the very essence of moral education. One might go so far as to say that psychic tension created by clashing ideas, systems of thought, and points-of-view may be the very essence of educational growth in general.

No other teaching medium holds greater potential for creating healthy learning tension than drama holds. Role-playing and improvisational activities permit students to do more than intellectualize about ideas, moral values, and issues. Such activities enable students to probe the depths of feeling which are inherent in tense, dramatic situations. To think and to feel as real characters in a real mess can stimulate moral growth. In addition, educational drama enables teachers to use, rather than to lament, the kinesthetic qualities of their students; it permits teachers to facilitate students' discovery of certain qualities about themselves; it encourages students to think critically and creatively; and it aids students' acquisition of other basic skills, such as reading, writing, speaking, listening, and viewing.

The teacher who is interested in both moral development and educational drama must be willing to take risks, to allow students to assert themselves in the classroom, and to be patient enough for the learning process to occur gradually, sometimes snail-like in its pace. The teacher must also be willing for students to engage in problem-solving activity, which leads to self-discovery and to the achievement of higher stages of growth.

Dramatic Material and Activities for Moral Development

If the teacher wishes to tie literary study to educational

drama for moral development, almost unlimited material exists. Edwin Arlington Robinson's poem "Miniver Cheevy" provides one example. Miniver is a man-child of the past, who sees himself as a "child of scorn." His mind-set is locked on nostalgia for "the days of old." The poem ends with an expression of Miniver's inability to cope with what he perceives as decadence in the modern world: "Miniver Cheevy, born too late/ Scratched his head and kept on thinking/ Miniver coughed, and called it fate/ And kept on drinking." Because the problems he faces bring him excruciating pain--the pain of modern recognition--Miniver escapes through drink. It is not Miniver's drinking which is the moral issue here; rather, it is his decision not to confront the problems he faces. He chooses not to cope with them because coping causes him too much pain.

To engage students in dramatizing this poem for the purpose of analyzing Miniver's moral behavior, the teacher can solicit answers from students to questions like the following:

What might be the setting in this poem? (Perhaps a bar in Miniver's own home.)

Which possible setting is likely to contain the most people? (Perhaps a private party or a public tavern.)

Who might be present if we say the setting is a public place? (Workers, local citizens, strangers passing through, etc.)

We now need characters. Who would like to discover what it is to be Miniver? Who will be Miniver's waiter, or bartender?

Everyone else can be anyone he/she chooses to be. Can you name the types of people you wish to be?

Now, what would everyone be doing in this public place when Miniver walks in?

What would Miniver do when he walks in, and whom might he engage in conversation?

At this point, the drama might begin, first with the creation of a setting and with characters taking their places. Much dialogue will be going on through separate conversations as Miniver enters. The students must be allowed to find their own direction as the drama develops. No one can know what might happen; however, the teacher must intrude occasionally to aid in moving the drama along when it lags. The teacher must guarantee success by rescuing students from situations which they are unable to handle. The teacher must sometimes stop the action to consider the level of seriousness of the actors and of the action, to suggest directions that the drama might take, and perhaps to assume a role himself/herself. At the appropriate stopping place, not only will students consider the quality of the drama and the feelings they experienced, but they will also consider Miniver's stage of moral reasoning. The same procedures apply to the remainder of these suggestions for materials and activities.

Virginia Woolf's short story "The Duchess and the Jeweller" presents the character of Oliver Bacon, whose moral reasoning is at stage 2 ("you scratch my back and I'll scratch yours"). Oliver is an insecure, self-made, wealthy jeweler, who has a chance to buy ten pearls for the price of 10,000 pounds sterling. He has reservations about paying such an exorbitant sum, but he decides to pay it anyway when the owner of the pearls--a Duchess--invites him to a prestigious dinner party. Because he is driven by an urge to achieve social status, he violates his better judgment and buys the jewels. Through his effort to "buy" social status, he sustains a substantial loss of money. Role playing this story provides opportunities for all students to participate (the dinner party scene); also, the situation provides an opportunity for students to analyze Oliver's moral reasoning.

Much of Clyde Griffiths' moral reasoning in Theodore Dreiser's An American Tragedy illustrates stage-3 behavior (one earns approval by having good intentions and by being "nice"). Throughout the novel, Clyde becomes increasingly conscious of what it takes to win approval. He attempts to do all that is necessary to be approved by his peers and by his superiors. He recognizes the need to wear the "right" clothes, talk the "right" language, and do the "right" things. He wins the approval of a wealthy young heiress, but--unfortunately for him--a lower-class girl, with whom he has had a romance, becomes pregnant. He considers murdering the girl, Roberta, but, at the last minute, he has doubts. He takes her out on the water in a small boat, and Roberta drowns. Did Clyde murder Roberta? At the end, Clyde is left only with doubts and his sense of "good intentions." He finally is tried and sentenced to death. A courtroom drama, based upon the one in Dreiser's novel, would ensure total student involvement and an analysis of Clyde's stage of moral development.

The fence-builder in Robert Frost's "Mending Wall" provides an example of stage-4 reasoning (law and order orientation). The wall-builder's invocation of the axiom, "Good fences make good neighbors," reveals a blind acceptance of tradition, which one must naturally respect and maintain for its own sake. After a reading of the poem, students might attempt to understand the fence-builder's reasoning by simulating a New England town meeting to discuss whether or not the wall should stand.

J. D. Salinger's The Catcher in the Rye depicts Holden Caulfield as one whose moral development has reached stage 5 (social-contract legalistic orientation). The sensitive person, who possesses a strong sense of individual conscience, often operates at this level, with an understanding of the laws and social principles which he/she is willing to accept. After much intellectual and spiritual agony, Holden ultimately recognizes and accepts the necessity to make his own kind of peace within certain conventions and institutions of the existing social order. Students can enact a drama in Holden's hospital room, where he is recovering from tuberculosis. Friends and family might visit him, engaging in conversations about the moral dilemmas he has faced and will face again.

Stage-6 behavior (universal ethical principle orientation) can be presented by such familiar literary works as Mark Twain's The Adventures of Huckleberry Finn, in which Huck, after arriving at a decision to help Jim escape from slavery, declares, "People would call me a low down Abolitionist and despise me for keeping mum--but that don't make no difference. I ain't a-going to tell"; Harper Lee's To Kill a Mockingbird, in which a lawyer, Atticus Finch, defends a black man in the deep South, despite vicious abuse from prejudiced citizens; Sophocles' Antigone, in which Antigone disobeys a direct order by King Creon and buries her brother, Polyneices, out of obedience to the law of "Heaven"; Joseph Conrad's The Secret Sharer, in which a ship's captain, obeying the dictates of his conscience, prepares for a fugitive's escape, realizing full well the possible consequences of his actions; and Henry David Thoreau's essay on Civil Disobedience, in which Thoreau advocates disobedience of unjust laws through such acts as refusing allegiance to an unjust state, ignoring unjust bills, and declaring personal war on social corruption. Each of these examples contains the "stuff" of high dramatic tension. Students, with skillful guidance and inquiry by teachers, can creatively enact any of these works for purposes of analyzing moral reasoning and of developing their own.

Kohlberg and Turiel define the teacher's task in facilitating moral development as helping a student to "(1) focus on genuine moral conflicts; (2) think about the reasoning he uses in solving such conflicts; (3) see inconsistencies and inadequacies in his way of thinking; and (4) find means of resolving such inconsistencies and inadequacies."[12] Further, they believe, teachers must "(1) have knowledge of the child's level of thought; (2) match the child's level by communicating at the level directly above; (3) focus on reasoning; and (4) help the child experience the type of conflict that leads to an awareness of the greater adequacy of the next stage."[13] Educational drama is eminently useful in helping teachers perform these tasks.

In order to find a student's particular stage of reasoning, Kohlberg and Turiel report on the use of the following dilemma:

> The drug didn't work, and there was no other treatment known to medicine which could save Heinz's wife, so the doctor knew that she had only about six months to live. She was in terrible pain, but she was so weak that a good dose of pain-killer like either ether or morphine would make her die sooner. She was delirious and almost crazy with pain, and in her calm periods, she would ask the doctor to give her enough to kill her. She said she couldn't stand the pain and that she was going to die in a few months anyway.
>
> Should the doctor do what she asks and give her the drug that will make her die? Why?[14]

Through the use of such moral dilemmas, it is possible for teachers to diagnose students' stages of moral development. Based upon such diagnoses, teachers can present possibilities for dramatic activities that occur one stage above the diagnosed stage of the student. Obviously, descriptions of moral dilemmas can themselves be dramatically enacted by students. Another example of a moral dilemma, used by Kohlberg and Turiel, follows:

> Before the civil war, we had laws that allowed slavery. According to the law, if a slave escaped he had to be returned to his owner like a runaway horse. Some people who didn't believe in slavery disobeyed the law and hid the runaway slaves and helped them to escape. Were they doing wrong or right?[15]

Students' responses to such dilemmas can come through treating the dilemmas as open-ended stories, with students called upon to debate the issues or to bring the dilemmas to tentative conclusions through dramatic involvement.

Another possibility for stimulating moral development through educational drama is the story of the Kentucky, or Beauchamp, tragedy. This story also provides an opportunity to teach the concept of chivalry in the Confederate South. It contains elements of several profound moral dilemmas which students can explore and understand through dramatization. The episode became common literary material which produced a number of novels and plays. It also has served as a measuring point of changing values in the South. Thomas Holly Chivers wrote a play about the Beauchamp tragedy called Conrad and Eudora (1834). Edgar Allan Poe wrote an unfinished play about it called Politian (1835). In the same year, Charlotte Conner Barnes wrote Octavia Brigaldi about the episode. Other works include novels by William Gilmore Simms, Beauchampe (1832) and Charlemont (1856); Hannah D. Pittman's The Heart of Kentucky (1908); Robert Penn Warren's World Enough and Time (1950); and Joseph Shearing's To Bed at Noon (1951).

For a full account of Beauchamp's story, one can read The Kentucky Tragedy; A Problem in Romantic Attitudes, edited by Loren J. Kallsen (New York: Bobbs-Merrill, 1963). Briefly, the story goes that in the 1820's Ann Cooke and a prominent lawyer named Solomon Sharp were involved in a romance. When it ended, Ann felt her honor was at stake, and she asked a young law student, acquainted with Sharp, to avenge her. Jereboam Beauchamp, the student, challenged Sharp to a duel, but Sharp refused. Ann and Jereboam were married, and Sharp ran for political office. During the campaign, Sharp's former romance with Ann was publicized, and Beauchamp subsequently stabbed Sharp to death in Frankfort, Kentucky. Beauchamp invoked the chivalric code--the code of honor--to justify his deed, but he was sentenced to hang. He and Ann made a suicide pact, and Ann succeeded in taking her life; however, Beauchamp failed and died on the gallows.

Obviously, the story contains many sub-plots for dramatic exploration. It also contains several moral dilemmas. Why did Beauchamp decide to challenge Sharp to a duel? Why did Ann urge him to do so? Why did Sharp refuse? Why did Beauchamp eventually kill Sharp? Why did Ann and Jereboam make a suicide pact? Is suicide a moral issue? What *are* the moral issues here? These are representative questions around which many dramatic activities can be structured to examine moral dilemmas and moral decision-making.

Finally, the story of Watergate, compellingly reported in Carl Bernstein's and Bob Woodward's *All the President's Men*, presents fertile territory for educational drama in the classroom. Seemingly unlimited material exists in this episodic account of political corruption for students to probe and to analyze moral dilemmas. Scores of characters and scores of tense human relationships in the Watergate story can provide challenging and provocative role-playing and improvisational activities for students to work through. Telephone conversations, personal interviews, clandestine meetings, editorial confrontations, public outrage, and various discussions between and among figures in the Watergate affair are some examples. Must one always obey authoritative orders? What does it mean to lose one's "moral compass"? What would you do if you were told to transfer "campaign funds" into a secret account for undetermined or "suspicious" purposes? Is it ever right to commit a "criminal act"? What *is* a "criminal act"? The Watergate story will continue to be relevant in the future, and the issues it represents can well serve teaching for moral development.

Conclusion

In light of many people's frustrations over the educational process today, and in light of increasing disillusionment over the effects which schools have on students, educational drama offers exciting potential for "turning school around." It ensures active involvement by students in the classroom, and it contributes to their personal growth. In giving advice to teachers about using drama as a method of instruction, Dorothy Heathcote says the following:

> And so automatically if you venture into drama as education, you are on this terrible road from the unselective to the classic, the highly selective, self-understanding as far as you can, all the time. When the children come into the classroom they are not totally unselective, but out of that mass of experience, attitude, environment (usually not the one you know much about these days, because we live in another place than where we teach) we begin this gradual process whereby the children may become more and more deeply, significantly, selective, in the cosmic order. Because nothing less than that is worth bothering about.
>
> So that is what somehow we have got to find a way of making into drama as education. Can we use it to edify? To draw attention to? To extend the understanding about? To bring about behavioural change? To help people develop gumption? To extend one's range of attitudes?[16]

The answers to Heathcote's questions have profound implications in teaching for moral development. Working to stimulate moral growth must become a top priority in modern education. And what is moral growth? According to Irving Kristol, it is getting young people "to have feelings about morality: to be morally sensitive and 'morally aware'?"[17] Developing "moral awareness is necessary to achieving a strong sense of self-respect, which, in turn, is necessary to developing respect for others. In the modern world, global survival depends upon mutual respect.

References

1"The Role of the School in Moral Development," in Moral Development: Proceedings of the 1974 ETS Invitational Conference (Princeton, N.J.: Educational Testing Service, 1974), p. 76.

2For a comprehensive study of Freud's theories, see particularly his A General Introduction to Psychoanalysis (New York: Liveright, 1935).

[3]See Piaget's *Science of Education and the Psychology of the Child* (New York: Orion Press, 1970). Also, see his *The Origins of Intelligence in Children* (New York: International University Press, 1952). For Piaget on moral development, see his *The Moral Judgment of the Child* (Glencoe, Ill.: Free Press, 1948).

[4]"Moral Development and Moral Education," in Gerald S. Lesser, ed., *Psychology and Educational Practice* (Glenview, Ill.: Scott, Foresman, 1971), pp. 410-465. See also Kohlberg's and Carol Gilligan's "The Adolescent as Philosopher: The Discovery of the Self in a Postconventional World," *Daedalus*, 1971, 1051-1086. See also Kohlberg's "Stage and Sequence: The Cognitive-Developmental Approach to Socialization," in D. A. Goslin, ed., *Handbook of Socialization Theory and Research* (Chicago: Rand-McNally, 1969), pp. 347-480. Finally, see Kohlberg's "Stages of Moral Development as a Basis for Moral Education," in C. Beck and E. Sullivan, eds., *Moral Education* (Toronto: University of Toronto Press, 1970).

[5]Kohlberg and Turiel, p. 411.

[6]*Ibid.*, p. 430.

[7]*Ibid.*, pp. 414-416.

[8]*Drama: What Is Happening* (Urbana, Ill.: National Council of Teachers of English, 1967), p. 1.

[9]*Explorations in the Teaching of Secondary English* (New York: Dodd, Mead, 1974), p. 198.

[10]"Issues in the Measurement of Moral Development," in *Moral Development: Proceedings of the 1974 ETS Invitational Conference* (Princeton, N.J.: Educational Testing Service, 1974), p. 67.

[11]Loeinger, p. 67.

[12]Kohlberg and Turiel, p. 454.

[13]*Ibid.*, p. 455.

[14]*Ibid.*, p. 434.

[15]*Ibid.*, p. 444.

[16]"Drama as Education," in New Destinations: The Cockpit Lectures, 17 January 1976 (London: Greater London Arts Association, 1976), p. 10.

[17]"Moral and Ethical Development in a Democratic Society," in Moral Development (see reference 10), p. 4.

EDUCATIONAL DRAMA AND THE BASICS

Jan A. Guffin

Not long ago, the term "basics" was understood by many to mean cognitive development only, specifically, the acquisition of skills in reading, spelling, writing, and mathematics. Today this term has been expanded to mean more than cognitive growth: depending on its context, it may mean anything from learning the skills necessary to balance a checkbook or change a tire, to developing a technique for solving personal and social problems or determining the role of the individual in a world characterized by both microcosmic and macrocosmic realities. For some, the term suggests going back; for others, it clearly means going forward.

Not long ago, too, educational drama was practiced by relatively few people. It meant something very specific: creative drama for elementary and junior high school children. It involved pantomime for beginners and improvisational play-acting for intermediate and advanced students. It drew heavily from literature for substance. Its purpose was to enable children to integrate the literary experience and articulate their understanding of dramatic situations and literary characters. It deliberately fostered an appreciation of dramatic art.

Today it is practiced by many and means many things. Although it has retained the original elements of mime and improvisation, it has extended its range of activities to include among others role-playing, dance-drama, and sociodrama; it has expanded its scope of subject matter to include history, sociology, anthropology, art, music, science--in fact, nearly every facet of the curriculum--and it has broadened its purpose not only to cultivate an appreciation of drama and the act of visualizing through dramatic means, but also to further both cognitive growth and personality development.

The relationship between educational drama and the basics, then, depends on the meanings assigned to each term. In the present context, I shall attempt to define basics from two points of view--the practical and the philosophical--and then explore the possibilities for acquiring the basics through various approaches to educational drama.

PRACTICAL CONCERNS

The much publicized results of the National Assessments of Educational Progress since 1969-70, the decline in scores on standardized tests during the past decade, and the ramifications of such events as the Peter Doe case, have raised public concern for the basics to a critical level. Educators, in turn, have refocused their efforts on teaching school children to read, to write, and to speak clearly and meaningfully. And although it may seem pointless, as Harold Shane suggests,[1] to argue the need to go back to such "old" basics, since their virtues are already recognized, it is nonetheless still a problem for the classroom teacher to devise meaningful ways for students to acquire skills in such areas.

The problem faced by the classroom teacher is at least two-fold: not only must he teach the acquisition of skills in the basic academic disciplines, but also he must determine ways to integrate, interrelate, and maintain such skills across a wide range of subjects at various grade levels. Since drama has been recognized throughout our century as the most integrated of the arts,[2] its promise for the teacher concerned with basics is manifold.

Before considering approaches to the teaching of basics through educational drama, however, the teacher must determine precisely what skills he wishes to emphasize. In doing so, he may discover that many of the concerns with which he customarily deals in the teaching of reading, the teaching of writing, the teaching of listening, and the teaching of speaking, do not vary significantly from one aspect of language arts to another. For example, all students attempting to become better readers, writers, listeners, or speakers, are consistently coping with their ability to perceive relationships and to increase their language growth.[3]

More specifically, both reading comprehension and the process of composing, though they may represent such process extremes as decoding and encoding, rely heavily on the ability to recognize and manage the following kinds of relationships: enumerative, sequential, spatial, comparative, and causal. The teacher of educational drama may capitalize on such needs by integrating these reading and writing skills in dramatics exercises. Below are several examples of classroom exercises which may be used either to introduce or reinforce the kinds of relationships named above:

Enumerative: Select three or four large-size posters with simple but vivid and contrastive color schemes. Ask the students to enumerate the colors seen in one poster, then another, and so on, by pantomiming or by reproducing sounds which depict the emotional qualities of the colors.

Or, divide the class into small groups and ask each group to enumerate the colors found in the clothing of their group by dramatizing each color. Conclude the exercise in whole-group instruction by creating a class story using volunteer colors from each group.

Sequential: Show the students a short film with a clearly defined sequence. Drummerhoff (Weston Woods, 1969, 6 min., color) is excellent, since it uses military rank to tell its story. After the students have viewed the film once, perhaps twice, and have developed an understanding of the sequence illustrated visually, ask them to create a dramatic situation with the class which employs the same kind of sequence but with different characters, such as the king, the queen, the courtiers, the servants, or the cooks; or the coach, the captain of the team, the team members, the cheerleaders, and the spectators. Any scheme of individuals which can be represented in a logical sequence will serve to reinforce the idea of order illustrated initially by the film and will enable students to see analogous relationships in both their reading and their everyday lives.

Spatial: Create a "hands-on" classroom experience by asking students to arrange the furniture in the classroom in ways which will depict various spatial relationships, such as high/low, near/far, or around/through. Then ask students to designate geographical equivalents for their arrangements, such as mountains, valleys, and rivers. Invite volunteers to select an occupation which they feel is appropriate to a given location in space and pantomime that occupation for the class. Repeat according to the number of volunteers.

For a variation of this exercise, invite students to dramatize social groups which are common to a given locale, such as mountaineers, fishermen, or farmers. What modes of employment and recreation are available to such people and what possibilities do they offer for dramatic enactment?

Comparative and Contrastive: Generally, students in a given school setting share many common characteristics in terms of lifestyle: their daily routines, their neighborhoods, their parents, their games and hobbies, their pets, their television habits. The perceptive teacher may determine the most common strands of interest or lifestyle and maximize the commonality of the group by challenging students to dramatize such similarities. Divide the class into four or five groups, for example, and ask each group to analyze a neighboring group for such similarities. Then give them three minutes of class time to reveal their findings in an improvisational presentation before the class. This may be done either in mime or in dialogue. Ask the class to guess answers.

A good way to point up contrastive relationships is to turn the entire class into dogs or cats and then challenge them to reveal their individuality through characteristic behavior. In other words, even though a dog is a dog, what makes him special? Some students may be owners, others, pets: reverse roles and explore a new kind of behavior.

Causal: Present students with a series of sentences which describe effects, such as "The neighbor's car has seen better days," "At first we thought the baby had swallowed poison, but we discovered it was only...," or "How could the cat possibly be covered with grape jelly, we wondered." Then ask students to construct the events which led to this effect.

Or give students a series of events (effects) and ask them to determine the causes. Minute mysteries are excellent for this kind of exercise.

Vocabulary Skills

Too often, vocabulary development is reduced simply to the acquisition of new words. Vocabulary development is that, of course, but the acquisition of new words represents only a part of language development. Stewig lists three important aspects of language development which have strong implications for the teacher of educational drama: vocabulary growth, paralanguage, and kinesics.[4] These categories include not only the learning of new word meanings, but also the manipulation of the voice through pitch, stress, and juncture (paralanguage), and the creation and control of gesture (kinesics) in articulating those meanings.

An additional consideration for the teacher to make concerns the process by which such skills are acquired. Piaget concluded that logic, or thinking in the largest sense, precedes language, and that in thinking "we have to do the work ourselves, making the connections, even if people take pains to point out to us connections that they have been able to make."[5] We arrive at language by meaningfully representing the world through various means, such as play, dreams, and imitation. Language is but another, more sophisticated way, then, of representing the world as we perceive it. Duckworth concludes from Piaget's findings that people get better at thinking by thinking and that they acquire language as they need it: a widening range of experiences produces richer levels of thought, which, in turn, produce a need for a broader range of vocabulary.[6]

A current study at Yale University reinforces this notion and carries somewhat stronger implications concerning the importance of kinesics. In their research with infants, Keesen and Nelson have found that a child's cognitive processes are not miniature versions of the adult's. "Infants, unlike adults, do not seem to organize the environment on the basis of form and color; they seem to make a functional analysis of the world--what is movable, what is eatable, what is touchable...." They conclude that children "do not have an immature language cognitive system; but a nonverbal, highly detailed, cognitive 'script' for how things should unfold...."[7]

The researchers indicate that nonverbal systems are often as useful as language. "If we would consider the worth of such nonverbal knowledge, they feel, we could make knowing language less of a make-or-break situation for children. And, they believe, if we respect children who have problems with language for what they do know rather than label them deficient, we may be better able to determine why they are not verbally proficient."[8] Another estimate of the importance of kinesics in language development is that it may account for up to 55 percent of the meaning of a message.[9]

The potential of educational drama for developing these important aspects of language growth is immense. A systematic way for the teacher of educational drama to approach such learning is to consider at one end of a curriculum continuum the repertoire of experience which a student brings to the classroom; at the other end, the demands and the opportunities which reside in the subject matter being taught; and somewhere in the middle, the dramatic experiences which can synthesize these extremes through the creation of new experiences.

For example, Blake, in an analysis of what children most successfully write about, derived two broad categories which speak directly to the teacher of educational drama: in the first are those topics that are related to ongoing classroom experiences and involve the creation of stories, plays, dictionaries, poems, reports, and the like which are related to the subject matter at hand; in the second category are topics which stem from everyday experiences in students' lives. Possible topics include neighborhood sights, sounds, and smells, the trip to and from school, weekend activities, likes and dislikes, being ill, helping parents, going shopping or to the doctor or dentist, the school, classroom, teachers, and visitors, older and younger children or relatives, early memories, hopes and fears, friends, favorite rooms or places, moving, pets and hobbies, visits, seasonal and nighttime changes, the weather, people's jobs, and special occasions.[10]

Words, new words of all kinds, of course, are bound to emerge in the dramatization of any kind of activity, and if the teacher is consciously drawing from both the subject matter and the experience of the student, the possibility for language growth is imminent. If the teacher wishes to be even more selective in what words should be taught, he may wish to consult Harold Herber's Success with Words,[11] which cross-references the basic vocabularies of English, mathematics, science and social studies.

The following activities are offered as examples of how the teacher might rely on dramatics activities of one kind or another to integrate subject matter and experience in lieu of language development:

(1) Discuss with students words which reflect various personalities, such as pompous, dogmatic, complacent, devious, and so on. Then challenge them to create characters like Peter Pompous or Debbie Devious who are based on

people drawn from their own experience--someone in their neighborhood, someone among their relatives, or someone among their friends.

(2) After studying a chapter in history, compose with the students a list of basic words which describe the feelings of various classes of people. What words best describe the condition or the feelings of the working class, the aristocrat, the poor? Then improvise situations which depict such words.

(3) Ask students to make a list of words which are most often associated with special days such as Halloween, Thanksgiving, Christmas, Easter, or the Fourth of July. Then improvise situations which are not related to those special occasions but which depict the words which the class has used to characterize the holidays.

(4) Determine which words in a given subject are used most frequently--words such as government, democracy, constitution, biology, microscope, composition, stanza, theme, paraphrase. Give the students a list of the roots from which such words are built. Dramatize the roots in class as a way of visualizing the origin of such words and as a way of preparing the student to meet the root in related words.

(5) Ask students to select one individual in their daily lives whom they can monitor for one week to determine certain words which appear frequently in their speech pattern. At the end of the week, ask students to choose two working partners for an improvisational exercise. Then give the following assignment: "The three of you meet coincidentally in the supermarket (or shopping center--any of various places will do). Discuss your plans for a coming vacation by using the words which appeared with greatest frequency on your list."

(6) Give students contrastive sentences such as, "You are the best pet in the whole world and I don't know what I would do without you," and "You are the most ridiculous animal I have ever laid eyes on, and the quicker I can get rid of you, the better." Ask one student to play the owner, the other to play the dog. Ask the owner to deliver the sentences in a conventional way and watch the dog's reactions. Then ask him to deliver the pleasant sentence in a harsh tone, the harsh sentence in a pleasant tone, and watch the dog's reactions again. Discuss the importance of pitch, stress, and juncture in communicating to both animals and people.

(7) In The Belle of Amherst, Emily Dickinson is portrayed as saying, "Now, there's a word you take your hat off to!" Ask students to find a word they would "take their hat off to," then place their word in a hat, draw a word from the hat, discover its meaning, write the word on the board, and pantomime its meaning for the class.

(8) Improvise family situations in which students assume various roles at the dinner table. Ask each person at the table to express a variety of feelings in a non-verbal way. How might the father react to indicate his disapproval of a child's behavior at the table? How might the mother come to the child's defense? How might the child sulk or immediately straighten up and behave according to the father's wishes?

(9) Enumerate with the class the emotions felt by a character in a narrative, such as London's "To Build a Fire" or Bierce's "An Occurrence at Owl Creek Bridge." Try pantomiming those feelings in the order in which they occurred in the narrative.

(10) Ask students to observe with care another person watching a performance of some kind (a television show, a play, a lecture, a concert) to determine the non-verbal reactions of that individual. Reproduce them in pantomime for the class to see if classmates can guess (a) what kind of performance is being observed, and (b) what the overall feeling is on the part of the observer.

Listening Skills

Wilt made a comprehensive report of listening research during the last thirty years.[12] Among the objectives for listening which appear in her report are the following:

- to improve the ability to follow directions
- to maintain attention
- to analyze conversation and speech
- to listen to sounds of the language
- to listen to the context
- to mentally organize thoughts
- to distinguish between relevant and irrelevant information
- to listen for a purpose
- to determine main ideas and important details

to make comparisons
to determine normal sequence
to find inferences and draw conclusions
to sense emotions and moods.

She points out the similarities between such a list and a list of objectives in reading, then cautions the reader that however valuable such a list may be in helping the teacher understand what to cultivate, the isolation of such skills also tends toward oversimplification of the listening process.[13] She notes a strong trend in teaching English, however, to emphasize more and more oral language in our classrooms. "This is the thrust we believe will promote the teaching of good listening habits and skills. The evaluation of one's ability to listen can never be left to discrete tests of individual skills. The efficacy of listening will need to be found in observation of a person's ability to interact in a communication situation with all of its ramifications rather than in whether an individual can remember facts he hears."[14]

It may seem, then, that the teacher of educational drama could reasonably assume that the development of listening skills would be a concomitant of any dramatics exercises which focused on skills necessary for improved reading, writing, and language development. To some extent this will be true; however, the teacher cannot rely simply on the emotional involvement of the student to insure the development of good listening habits. Rather, listening for a purpose must be reinforced much of the time. Therefore, lessons which deal with various dramatics activities require reasonable follow-up activities involving student evaluation. When the student knows that he must ultimately make a judgment about a scene which has been improvised or an exercise in pantomime which has grown out of a previous assignment, his purpose for listening, and in turn, his accuracy increase substantially.

PHILOSOPHICAL CONCERNS

Up to this point, I have dealt with the acquisition of the kind of basic skills which I earlier suggested had been central to our curricula for many years, the basics which a number of people insist we get "back to." In the remainder of my discussion, I would like to devote attention to a different set of basics, the "new basics" which others are suggesting American education should move forward to. Feeling is strong enough about such new basics that writers ranging from those concerned with the philosophy of education in general to those concerned with the philosophy of teaching English in particular have found much to say on the subject.

Shane suggests that it is relevant to "move on to new and additional basic skills which the next 25 years will require of youth."[15] He elaborates as follows: "Certainly cross-cultural understanding and empathy have become fundamental skills, as have the skills of human relations and intercultural rapport. In local, national, and world settings that require the arts of compromise and reconciliation, of consensus building, and of planning for interdependence, a command of these talents becomes 'basic'--from the level of town meetings to the Assembly of the United Nations. Anticipation of future events and their possible consequences, as well as the ability to effect desirable outcomes, also are important learned behaviors. It is toward such 'new fundamentals' in addition to the three Rs, that we need to direct our energies. The very process of doing so should effectively lend new meaning, motivation, and purpose to mastery of the substantive content of instruction."[16]

Shane's observations are both reinforced and refined somewhat by the findings of a Task Force on Graduation Requirements appointed by the National Association of Secondary School Principals. This task force noted a trend among local school districts which were attempting to respond to the public determination to define the American high school diploma: literacy is coming to mean more than a functional understanding of the three Rs; it is coming to mean also an ability to function as a contributive citizen in a rapidly changing environment. It concluded that diploma requirements should therefore include the following verified attributes of the graduates: an ability to read, write, and compute with specified proficiency; an acquaintanceship with the American experience, to include an understanding of the process and structure of democratic governance; and the successful completion of a series of courses and/or planned experiences, some of which involve a group setting.[17]

Attempts by various school districts to hold themselves accountable for such an education have led to the use of competency-based education and a wider use of criterion-referenced testing. Oregon has become a model for schools interested in attempting such programs. The state in 1973 designed twenty areas of personal, social and career development as necessary to survival in modern life. These areas become a part of the requirements for a diploma beginning with the class of 1978. Competency is demonstrated in each of the twenty areas, but the level of competency is determined locally by each district."[18]

A representation of the Oregon Plan will illustrate the attempt to combine the "old" and the "new" basics into a kind of education which heretofore has been merely presumed. The twenty areas of minimum survival-level competencies are as follows:

> Personal Development: To survive and grow as an individual, Oregon believes it is necessary to develop (a) basic skills--reading, writing, computing, listening, speaking, and analyzing, (b) understanding scientific and technological processes, (c) understanding the principles involved to maintain a healthy mind and body, (d) the skills to remain a lifelong learner.
>
> Social Responsibility: Good citizenship requires the ability to cope responsibly (a) with local and state government as well as national government, (b) in personal interactions with the environment, (c) on the streets and highways, (d) as a consumer of goods and services.
>
> Career Development: To survive and advance in any career area, students are asked to develop (a) entry-level skills for their chosen career fields, (b) good work habits and attitudes, (c) the ability to maintain good interpersonal relationships, (d) the ability to make appropriate career decisions.[19]

Such developments in general education are not inconsistent with the trend in English education to attempt to humanize the curriculum. Volumes have been written since the 1966 Dartmouth Conference explaining why and how the language arts curriculum must be altered to meet the needs of students in a fast-changing world. In post-Dartmouth research conducted by Farrell for the National Council of Teachers of English, some speculations were made concerning the responsibilities for the teacher of English between 1970 and the year 2000.[20] Farrell is careful to state the limitations of his findings: "The generalizations derive their support, unless they contain a negation, from items receiving 40 percent of higher probability of being implemented. Since no item on any questionnaire received 100 or even 80 percent probability of implementation, all generalizations are highly conditional."[21]

Despite these limitations, the findings of his study are more often than not commensurate with subsequent developments such as those described above. For example, among the items listed concerning the future secondary curriculum are the following:

> (1) The curriculum will include new content as well as new arrangements of old content.
>
> (2) There will be increased emphasis upon both individualized instruction and problem-solving approaches to learning.... Less emphasis will be placed on students' learning facts than upon their learning skills of inquiry and methods both of solving problems and of managing information. A common means of teaching at least some of these skills and methods will be games and simulations.
>
> (3) Despite increased participation by industry in the production, maintenance, and use of instructional materials, curricular stress upon human relations will be greater than it is at present--on ways of adjusting conflicts, on relations of minority groups to each other and to the majority, on literature that reflects great human problems, on materials in the social studies that focus on the enhancement of the individual, etc.[22]

Farrell's study also speculates on the changes which may be rendered in English as a subject:

> (1) The curriculum in English will be more flexible, its objectives and means of evaluation more clearly defined, its emphasis more upon process than upon content.
>
> (2) ... English will be stressed as an instrument for clarifying social and personal experiences and students will participate in classroom dramatics activities: acting out plays, role-playing, improvising drama. By the end of the century, the global concept of creative thinking may have been broken down into its component skills, with the conditions for the learning of these skills defined.

> (3) More attention will be paid to processes underlying written and oral composition.... Particular emphasis will be given to psychological matter (analyzing audience, establishing voice, etc.) and thought processes underlying writing and speaking.[23]

However speculative the new basics may be, and however much we may strive to maintain the old basics, we can be reasonably sure that change is inevitable. No teacher is in a more auspicious position to participate in constructive change than the teacher of educational drama. One who understands the residual powers in dramatics activities for integrating personal and academic experiences, for interrelating subject areas, and for contributing to the personal and social growth of the individual cannot help viewing such change with excitement.

Although leading British and American proponents of educational drama, such as Winifred Ward, Brian Way, and Dorothy Heathcote, differ somewhat in their approach to working with students, they tend to agree with the following statement by Way: "Indeed, it is true to say that drama, so far from being new is closely interwoven in the practical implementation of both the spirit and substance of every Education Act ever passed, especially the idea of the development of the whole child. But it must be this whole person upon whom our concentration is centered; to make drama another subject in an overcrowded curriculum is to shift the emphasis away from the many 'whole persons' to drama itself."[24]

Without minimizing either the Ward or the Heathcote approach to educational drama, I would like to focus on Way's approach for its relevance to the synthesis of what we have identified here as the "old" and "new" basics. In his book, Development Through Drama,[25] which is now gaining wide use in the United States, Way first establishes the theoretical basis for his approach and then deals with the implementation of his ideas in a series of carefully planned activities focusing on various aspects of improvisational drama, such as concentration, imagination, movement and sound, speaking, sensitivity and characterization, improvisation, the importance of space, and social drama.

Like Ward and Heathcote, he is concerned with such concomitant aspects of improvisational drama as the increase of critical thinking, the creative use of individual resources, a growing social and aesthetic awareness, etc., but he is perhaps more concerned with the process which lies beneath the entire range of improvisational acts. At the center of this process, he identifies seven constituents: concentration, the senses, imagination, physical self, speech, emotion, and intellect.[26]

Since these constituents vary in degree in relation to chronological age, mental age, and emotional maturity, Way denies the possibility of grading his exercises according to any age group or of developing anything like a linear curriculum in creative drama. Accordingly, it becomes the responsibility of the teacher or leader of creative drama to assess the readiness of his pupils in all of these areas, and, starting at whatever point seems most appropriate, to further develop each of these constituents. Ultimately, Way regards the development of the individual as that which moves from an egocentric level, where the focus is on harnessing individual resources and putting the individual in control of them, to an ethnocentric level, where individuals will harmonize their resources with their physical and social environment.[27]

As we consider the possibilities of educational drama in teaching whatever the new basics become, the following observations are worthy of consideration.

<u>At the Personal Level</u>:

> (1) A school is good when it includes self-knowledge as part of its definition of worthwhile knowledge. In a good school, a student's feelings are not considered an intrusion upon his pursuit of knowledge, but a subject of inquiry themselves. Although a good school need not become a psychiatric hospital, it should make a systematic effort to help a student understand himself, get in touch with his own feelings, monitor his own behavior, and so on.[28]

> (2) Young people today need a chance to get acquainted with themselves, deep down inside. They need to try on for size different kinds of ideas. They need perspective to see that the human problems they are wrestling with are old in time, though perhaps different in form. They need to become aware of the shining visions of the best of the world's thinkers, dreamers, and moral leaders. They need time to test these ideas, largely by talking about them with their peers.[29]

At the Social Level:

(1) Common and recurring interactions involving social entities--that is, individuals, groups, organizations, or nations--include conflict, compromise, threat, punishment, promise, reward, influence, force, and violence. A useful framework for analysis can be constructed by isolating three kinds of elements: the actors (nations, groups, peoples), the relations or social processes involved (conflict, cooperation), and judgments about power (strong-weak), morality (good-bad), and change (status-quo-alteration).[30]

(2) The media provide a supply of data each day. The scope and variety are such that no one means of selection seems likely to be satisfactory. The data in the international affairs field are endless. There are more than 150 countries, each with a history, political and economic characteristics, and cultural settings. Almost any information about countries, relationships, and settings could be important.[31]

(3) Creative problem-solving, which involves the collective brainstorming, evaluation, and implementation of ideas, is successful with students at every socio-economic level.[32]

At the Career Development Level:

(1) Schools desperately need ways of getting children and youths acquainted with wide areas of the world of work. Starting in kindergarten and climaxing in the junior high school years, where plans begin to crystallize, they need an ongoing, attractive, informative program.[33] The possibilities of visualizing such experiences are legion in educational drama.

(2) Consumer education needs to be backed by competence. Schools can help children and youth learn the practical arts of effective shopping and buying. They can inoculate young people against the wiles of shady advertising and labeling. They can help them to identify honest, competent merchants and salespeople, and get maximum help from them in generally pleasant relationships. They can teach

young people to budget and manage their money, to use credit wisely, and to get the insurance that meets their needs.[34]

Deciding what to teach and how to teach it is, of course, not new. However, it is more complicated than ever before. The teacher who is willing to tackle these problems as we approach the last quarter of the century will judiciously identify both the basic skills which need to be maintained and those which need to be incorporated into the curriculum. Such a teacher also needs to acquaint him or herself with the ramifications of educational drama--the possibilities of self and group expression through the art of pantomime, improvisation, role-playing--and the processes which will most effectively implement such drama in the classroom.

References

[1]Harold G. Shane, "America's Next 25 Years: Some Implications for Education," Phi Delta Kappan 58 (September 1976), 78-83.

[2]This is a view held in common by such diverse educational figures as John Dewey (philosopher), Winifred Ward (educational drama leader), Hughes Mearns (artist-teacher), James Moffett (professor and language arts expert). It is explored in depth in Jan A. Guffin, "Winifred Ward: A Critical Biography," an unpublished Ph.D. dissertation, Duke University, 1976.

[3]See Eleanor Duckworth, "The Language and Thought of Piaget: And Some Comments on Learning to Spell," in Martha L. King, Robert Emans, and Patricia J. Cianciolo, eds., A Forum for Focus (Urbana, Ill.: National Council of Teachers of English, 1973), pp. 15-31; Miriam E. Wilt, "Listening! What's New?" ibid., pp. 63-72; and Stephen Dunning and Virginia Redd, "What Are the Basics?" Slate 1 (August 1976), 1-3.

[4]John Warren Stewig, "Creative Drama and Language Growth," in King, Emans, and Cianciolo, op. cit., pp. 237-50.

[5]Duckworth, op. cit., p. 18.

[6]Ibid., p. 26.

[7]Barbara Radloff, "What Does the Child's World Look Like?" Carnegie Quarterly 24 (spring 1976), 1-3.

[8]Ibid., p. 3.

[9]Albert Mehrabian and Susan R. Ferris, "Inference of Attitudes from Non-verbal Communication in Two Channels," Journal of Consulting Psychology 31 (June 1967), 251; cited by Stewig, op. cit., p. 247.

[10]Howard E. Blake, "What Children Write About," in King, Emans, Cianciolo, op. cit., pp. 175-177.

[11]Harold L. Herber, Success with Words (New York: Scholastic Book Services, 1973).

[12]Wilt, op. cit.

[13]Ibid., p. 69.

[14]Ibid.

[15]Shane, op. cit., pp. 82-83.

[16]Ibid., p. 83.

[17]James P. Clark and Scott D. Thomson, Competency Tests and Graduation Requirements (Reston, Va.: National Association of Secondary School Principals, 1976), p. 18.

[18]Ibid., p. 6.

[19]Ibid.

[20]Edmund J. Farrell, Deciding the Future: A Forecast of Responsibilities of Secondary Teachers of English, 1970-2000 A.D. (Urbana, Ill.: National Council of Teachers of English, 1971).

[21]Ibid., p. 154.

[22]Ibid., pp. 137-138.

[23]Ibid., pp. 154-157.

[24]Brian Way, Development Through Drama (London: Longman Group, 1967), p. 2.

[25] Ibid.

[26] Ibid., p. 7.

[27] Ibid., pp. 11-12.

[28] Neil Postman and Charles Weingartner, How to Recognize a Good School (Bloomington, Ind.: Phi Delta Kappa Educational Foundation, 1973), p. 34.

[29] Fred Wilhelms, What Should the Schools Teach? (Bloomington, Ind.: Phi Delta Kappa Educational Foundation, 1972), p. 38.

[30] James Becker, Education for a Global Society (Bloomington, Ind.: Phi Delta Kappa Educational Foundation, 1974), p. 37.

[31] Ibid., p. 36.

[32] E. Paul Torrance and J. Pansy Torrance, Is Creativity Teachable? (Bloomington, Ind.: Phi Delta Kappa Educational Foundation, 1973), p. 27.

[33] Wilhelms, op. cit., p. 18.

[34] Ibid., p. 19.

EDUCATIONAL DRAMA AND THE BRAIN'S RIGHT HEMISPHERE

Betty Jane Wagner

When educators get together to talk about the act of learning, they are more likely in this decade to describe the process in terms of hemispheric brain function than in Benjamin Bloom's taxonomies. Why is this? It is not because Bloom's distinctions between the cognitive, affective, and manipulative domains were not influential in their day nor because the spelling out of instructional objectives was not for many teachers a clarifying exercise. The reason is that merely identifying cognitive, affective, or manipulative outcomes seems a paltry goal when confronted with the potential of full human brain functioning or with actual divergent thinking with which students can astound their teachers. The morbid phrase, "identifying terminal behavior" which designers of programmed instruction have used to describe goal setting for a specific instructional activity is happily lapsing into disuse.[1]

Recent brain research is largely responsible for an expansion of our understanding of human sensory and cognitive equipment. This "research strongly suggests that our whole definition of human consciousness is severely limited."[2] Discoveries made in the process of splitting apart the brain's left and right hemispheres in the interest of reducing seizures for epileptic patients have revealed that each half of the human brain has a separate mode of cognition.[3] Moreover, each hemisphere is capable of functioning on its own. Probably the most amazing discovery is that if brain damage occurs early enough in a child's life, the undamaged hemisphere is able to take over the major functions of the other half of the brain. Thus, if a young child has his entire left hemisphere surgically removed, the right half can take over the management of the speech function that would have normally been the work of the left hemisphere. It would seem we have only a glimmer of understanding of how the human brain actually functions.

The implications of this brain research have yet to be taken account of by most educators. Jean Houston, a psychologist and director of the Foundation for Mind Research, speaks for many researchers who are convinced that we have not begun to educate our right or non-verbal brain hemisphere. "Our experiments persuade us that ordinary people, given opportunity and training, can learn to think, feel, and know in new ways, to become more imaginative, and to aspire within realistic limits to a much larger awareness."[4]

Split brain research has demonstrated that there is a kind of knowing that cannot be verbalized. For example, persons who have undergone surgery to split their brains can select with their left hands, from a sack full of fruit they can feel but not see, the appropriate fruit in answer to the question: "What does a monkey like to eat?" However, they will not be able to say the word "banana" unless they can see the fruit or feel it with their right hand. What is missing in a split brain is the connecting links to effect communication from one hemisphere to the other. However, the right hemisphere, which controls the left hand, knows what that hand is feeling even when it cannot share this information verbally. This fact about brain function poses a challenge for educators. We need to figure out strategies to expand the right hemisphere understanding in children without split brains so both their hemispheres can profit by it.

Our schools have traditionally been oriented toward the education of the left hemisphere, with a heavy emphasis on verbal behavior and linear, logical thinking. Children who are naturally spatial visualizers have a tougher time proving they know how to deal with the world than more verbal children do. Few opportunities are provided for them to learn in their right-brained way, and we tend to test primarily for left-brained functioning. Even Jean Piaget's pervasively influential studies in children's thinking were largely of left-hemispheric cognition. Robert Ornstein pleads, "If we agree that most present-day curriculums stimulate primarily the left brain, then we recognize the need for content, method, and materials that will utilize the right brain in an equally vigorous manner."[5]

Although split brain research is comparatively new, the idea of nonverbal education--what we now refer to as right-brained learning--has actually been around a long time. Perhaps the new research findings will give it the final nudge toward respectability and importance it needs to make a difference in how most educators think about learning and how they develop strategies for learning.

Charles Weingartner is one of many educators to decide that the time is right for the "new idea" of holistic, non-verbal learning to be taken seriously.

> The 'new idea' has to do with what Aldous Huxley called the 'non-verbal humanities,' which he explained by citing the ideas of John Dewey much earlier on, and especially Dewey's interest in the ideas of F. M. Alexander. This 'new idea,' then, has been around for sixty years or more; apparently it was 'ahead of its time.'
>
> The time for this 'new idea' may be right for a variety of reasons, including the changes that have occurred in the world during the last thirty years to which education, by and large, has yet to respond, and, more especially, recent information developed by research relating to brain function. The most formidable 'new frontier' left to explore is not the oceans, nor the womb, nor outer space, but 'inner space': the brain. As it turns out, the least known territory is between our own ears.[6]

Brain research has revealed that one half of the brain, the right hemisphere in most right-handed people, is responsible for assessing the body's orientation in space and for synthesis as a mode of knowing. In most left-handed people, the left hemisphere functions this way. The other half of the brain is responsible for speech and logic. As we have learned in physiology courses, the right hemisphere controls the actions of the left side of the body and vice versa. (Thus right-hemisphere functioning is sometimes referred to as "left-handed knowing."[7]) What we may not have learned in physiology is that two distinct modes of knowing are lodged in our brains, one in each hemisphere.

The functioning of the left hemisphere is easier to describe, for it can be verbalized. The way the right hemisphere operates seems more mysterious, for it is not accessible to speech or logic. This mode of knowing that we cannot ultimately and fully describe has been given many labels and characteristics, most of which allude to its inaccessibility. Here are some of those terms contrasted with a list of terms used to refer to left-brained functioning:

Left Brain	Right Brain
Reason	Intuition
Analysis	Synthesis
Rational	Metaphoric
Comparison and contrast	Holistic vision
Logic	Analogic
Verbal	Spatial visualizing
Speech	Music
More involved in time	More involved in space
Scientific	Primitive
Objective	Subjective
Outer	Inner
Information	Deep understanding
Linear	Cyclical
Sequential	Simultaneous
Detailed	Whole
Controlled	Creative
Idea	Image
Concept	Insight
Alert	Aware
Dominant	Spiritual
Employing steady input and accumulation of data	Attempting to develop another "organ of perception"
"Ordinary" realm of past, present, and future	Present-centered
Cause and effect	Patterned whole
Getting meaning	Discerning pattern
Knowing	Absorbing
Manipulating the outer world	Controlling inner space
Observing	Meditating
Active	Receptive
Clear	Subtle
Day	Night

The word intuition has long been used to refer to non-rational knowing. It is derived from the Latin in tueri, meaning "to enter inside." In Zen, kensho, a word used to describe enlightenment, literally means "to enter inside." In the Chinese philosophy of the I Ching the intuitive mode is called K'un, meaning "the receptive."[8]

Roberto Assagioli sees intuition as a psychic organ or means for apprehending reality. As a cognitive function it serves to synthesize "in the sense that it apprehends the totality of a given situation or psychological reality. It does not work from the part to the whole--as the analytical mind does--but apprehends a totality directly in its living existence. As it is a normal function of the human psyche, its activation is produced chiefly by eliminating the various obstacles preventing its activity."[9]

Intuitive knowing is not new, nor is its recognition. What is new is laboratory research that localizes this kind of non-verbal knowing in the brain's right hemisphere and the widespread concern of educators and therapists that this mode of knowing has too long been neglected in the United States. With the explosion of knowledge in this century has come a glut of information; in schools and out we are surrounded by more facts than our left hemispheres know what to do with. We need help. Bob Samples is one of the people reminding us that "our right hemisphere is ready to deal with the rational overload of contemporary times."[10]

Psychologists and psychiatrists are showing new interest in right-hemispheric function in the process of therapy. Two new forms of therapy--psychosynthesis and Gestalt--recognize this other mode of knowing. Unlike psychoanalysis, the goal in psychosynthesis is to balance the extremes of consciousness and to evoke the functioning of both intuition and intellect. In Gestalt therapy (not to be confused with Wolfgang Kohler's Gestalt psychology of the 1920's), participants are encouraged to stay in the present moment and "to become aware of their body language and therefore to bring their *whole* selves into consciousness."[11] Fritz Perls, who originated the Gestalt technique, notes, "Ultimate awareness can only take place if the computer [the thinking process] is gone, if the intuition, the awareness is so bright that one really comes to his senses."[12]

In addition to medical research on the brain itself and concern by educators and therapists that metaphoric knowing be taken seriously, there is in this country an increasing interest in and practice of transcendental meditation or yoga techniques for inner awareness. Despite the obvious trappings of a fad, the centering technique for inner enlightenment, seems, like the sexual revolution, to be one of the few developments to survive the excesses of the sixties. Much of what brain researchers have discovered in scientifically-controlled laboratory tests has given new credence to non-Western religious beliefs and practices. The mind and the body--even that supposedly autonomic nervous system--are more closely interrelated than has before been guessed by the Western mind.[13] There seems to be a demonstratable non-rational tional wisdom that can be tapped through certain techniques of focused awareness.

So what does all this have to do with educational drama? Simply this. Dramatic inventing, the improvisational mode of drama, often referred to as creative dramatics, is as dependent on right-brained as on left-brained functioning. Drama can begin only when the participants agree to believe that a certain set of conditions is defining their action. Only by this act of will--the will to believe by all who take part--is drama possible. This deliberate decision to believe is perhaps one of the clearest ways to contrast right-brained from left-brained function. One's senses bring the left hemisphere a picture of the real world or of what passes in the left hemisphere's logic for "the real world." We often say, "Seeing is believing." This is not the way the right hemisphere works. To become truly receptive, you have to believe before you can receive. In other words, believing is seeing. Awareness emerges as you consciously focus on the believed moment. To get themselves into a drama, many participants find bodily, especially rhythmic, movement helpful. Such activity focuses the attention in a state of relaxed concentration in much the same way as does the repetition of a mantra or the focus on a mandala or specially constructed visual image in yoga practice. By slowing sensory input and concentrating on believing that one can know in another mode, inner "seeing" becomes possible. The one demand that the art of drama relentlessly makes--even of the youngest of children--is to believe. "We are on a rocket to the moon"; "This is the middle of the hot and steamy jungle"; "On this hill we can catch our first scent of the sea"; "We have no one here to help us in this frozen waste but these dogs" and so on.

This is not to say that in drama participants really are transported to a make-believe world. Except for very young children, most persons who engage in dramatic invention have the heady experience of having it both ways. They both believe the drama and at the same time are clearly aware that it is their own invention. It is a group fantasy they have created together--something real and shared and at the same time something imagined and gossamer. At any moment, the dramatic web can be unspun and the participants can sit again in a concrete classroom. It is then they can use their left brains to reflect on the significance of what they have just created.

In drama, students expand their awareness by focusing their attention on a mutually agreed upon situation and selecting from their previous experience appropriate actions and feelings for that moment. As they fuse these actions and feelings with the challenge to invention that a tense dramatic moment evokes, they discover what they know. The effect can be arresting and exhilarating.

To see how this process of discovery through dramatic inventing works, let's look at a drama Dorothy Heathcote led recently. A group of nine- and ten-year-olds had decided to do a drama about a voyage into outer space. Most of the action took place on the rocket itself and among the ground-control crew. After a tense blast off, Heathcote looked around at the children who had been on the fringes of the main action and asked them what the day had been like for the rest of the community. It was then she learned that what had not looked like significant overt behavior had actually been a moment of expanded awareness for one girl. She had been in a role she had chosen as one of the astronaut's wives. In response to Heathcote's question she told the group that she had trouble getting through her usual morning routines. "I forgot to put butter on the twins' sandwiches because I was thinking about my husband and was feeling all upset."

Heathcote said, "Our feelings do seem to interfere with our actions sometimes," and then pressed for more depth: "Can you find language or words to tell us what you were feeling?"

"I'm not sure. I was mixed up sort of. I felt proud he was going and thought how the twins would see their Daddy kind of like a hero. I thought I'd better tell them, like Momma tells me, not to brag out loud, but just be glad inside that he's their Daddy. Then, suddenly, I felt sad and thought what if he doesn't come back? How awful it would be if they didn't have a big, wonderful Daddy at all. We'd miss him terrible. Our space here would be awful--like that out there. I can't really say what I felt. It was hollow and sort of achey. Then I wished the children would come home, and I went to the window to look out for them."

This girl had done more than use words to embody fleeting emotions: she had expressed a universal understanding. Her insight was the product of her metaphoric mind, the right hemisphere. Through entering, getting inside of, the experience, she intuited what it is like for anyone whose loved ones risk danger to make new discoveries.

The concept of a bicameral brain with hemispheres that function differently makes possible an interpretation of this child's unusually mature insight. She was not taught in any overt sense; rather she was thrust into a situation in which she had a chance to bring to bear those past experiences and feelings that were called for in this newly imagined situation. Her thinking was divergent; it could not possibly have been predicted in advance. No programmed materials could have been devised to assure "terminal behavior"[14] of that sort.

Defenders of educational drama have expended much energy futilely chasing down identifiable behaviors participants in drama should demonstrate.[15] The truth is that the most significant outcomes of drama may well be those that cannot be seen. Had the child who was the astronaut's wife simply sat reflectively instead of pantomiming the making of sandwiches and drinking coffee as she did, she still might have come up with the same insight. Experience does not have to be observable to be significant. What drama can do best may not be observable as behavior. Even if this girl had not been able to verbalize her new understanding, that is no guarantee that she had not experienced it.

This fact is, of course, going to be one that plagues those of us who have committed ourselves to building a case in our culture for educational drama. We are going to have to face the bracing challenge of educating the public that supports the schools to the validity of right-brained understanding. This kind of learning will not lend itself to easily-measurable student behavioral change; it will instead remain dark and inaccessible to left-brained accountability measuring devices. This is not to say that drama cannot be defended, however. More of us will simply have to take on the task of expanding cultural awareness of the two distinct modes of knowing--both of which are cognitive acts, functions of the human brain.

In the past, by using Bloom's taxonomies as a framework for analysis of the act of learning, we have unwittingly denigrated the importance of our feelings. Whenever anyone referred to the cognitive and the affective domains, it was clear which was important: the cognitive. All too often the assumption has been that the affective domain is useful as a means--or in arts education--but the important educational goal is cognitive mastery. For most teachers the education of the feelings has been considered less important or at least less appropriate as a school goal than education of the mind. We need only consider what kinds of learnings are reflected on standardized tests to remind us of the overwhelming value accorded mastery in the cognitive domain.

Bloom's taxonomies made it possible for an educator to conceive of a cognitive act as something apart from feeling. That is, of course, nonsense. To think is to feel as well. No idea is analyzed or toyed with in our left hemisphere that is not also responded to with puzzlement, intrigue, joy--in short, with feeling. We think about what interests us, and interest is a human attribute that would be categorized in Bloom's taxonomies as "affective." If left-hemisphered cognitive acts are accompanied by emotion, how much more are those acts of synthesis in the right hemisphere! The synthesis the astronaut's wife experienced was cognition shot through with the energizing force of identification. To identify is to open the door to intuition, to entering into; identification is an act that is both cognitive and affective. Thus, it is less than fruitful to try to separate learning into cognitive and affective categories. Rather, it is wise to see cognition as inevitably vitalized by feeling. The more fecund metaphor is the one born in the brain research laboratory: the image of the bicameral brain. Analysis and synthesis are the two modes of cognition. Both are affective; both are essential for human survival. They cannot be ranked in importance.

The experiences students have when fully involved in educational drama stubbornly remind us that what can be objectively measured and observed as behavioral change may not matter much. More lies between people than we can neatly categorize and test for. Life at bottom is a strange and wonder-filled affair, and only a right-brained vision that can synthesize and symbolize can complete the nourishment of students immersed in a left-brained culture.

Long before students can lucidly verbalize their experience, they are storing away in their right hemispheres actual and imagined experiences to reshuffle and order later in their left brains. The more evocative and tense the dramatic inventions they can experience and the more powerful the literature and art they can receive, the better they will be able to process future experience and achieve a synthesis that takes account of the fullness and complexity of human life.

To show how drama is uniquely suitable for evoking right-brained functioning, here is how a colleague, Ruth Tretbar, and I led a group of lively eight- and nine-year-olds in a drama that led to reflection in our Demonstration School at National College of Education. The idea for the focus of the drama was a moral dilemma that appeared in a newspaper account last fall.[16] The problem was this: a Brazilian tribe of Indians, whose culture has previously been isolated from that of the white man, was facing the coming of non-Indian strangers who were assigned the task of cutting down the trees in the Indians' valley at the headwaters of the Amazon River. This lumbering operation, which, of course had all the appropriate governmental permits and authorization, led to a confrontation with the tribe. When the Indians sensed that they would be defeated, they decided to kill their own babies rather than see them grow up under the domination of an alien culture. That culture was the one the lumbermen coming into their valley represented. The problem for the Brazilian governmental officials was, of course, to decide whether to intervene on the side of the law against murder or to let the tribe determine its own destiny. Certainly a problem of this magnitude stands in sharp contrast to the pablum all too often served up in commercial curriculum materials designed to modify student behavior in measurable but trivial ways. This moral dilemma, like all true human crises, was set in the matrix of age-old questions of value that underlies the group consciousness of any human community. It was a problem worthy of the attention of both hemispheres of the brain.

From the initial discussion with the class, it seemed clear that they were not going to even consider killing their own babies; nor were they really interested in the alternatives the white men faced--to intervene or not. Rather, they were eager to turn the drama into a stereotypical Indian war with the white man. By the end of the first session, the children were busy making elaborate plans for a battle to stop the lumbermen. Their will was engaged; they were sorry to run out of time before they could begin their fight.

When we met again a few days later, the children were as interested as ever in fighting. Although we were happy that they were ready to identify with the Indians rather than the whites, we were determined not to have the drama turn into a war. Instead, we wanted to see if we could help them understand with their metaphorical hemispheres what it would be like to be so pressed as a culture that you would even contemplate such an unconscionable act as participation in your own group's genocide. Because the class was in the throes of a long unit on water, and because we were dead set against leading them into a war, I changed the problem they faced from an encroachment by lumbermen to the building of a dam downriver from their valley. I decided that a gradual rising of the river would be harder to fight back with bows and arrows than would be teams of men with chain saws. So we began our drama on the banks of the river, fishing with the huge, sharpened spears the tribe had readied for their defense. The fishing was intense; as they worked, they talked about the problem of the white men building a dam on this sacred river. The rhythm of the act of fishing helped them focus their attention so their right brains could function more effectively. As a tribe member, I stayed in role and sat on the banks weaving a reed basket for the fresh fish. From this point on Ruth Tretbar and I stayed in role for nearly every minute of the next four drama sessions. We joined with the class in discovering what this tribe's response to this problem would be.

After everyone had had time to get into the task of fishing, Ashew, the tribe's chief, pulled out a fish that had 25 fins. All gathered around to look. Our witch doctor declared solemnly that this was a bad luck fish. Now we had a concrete object as a symbol for metaphoric minds to reflect on. What was to be done with this evil omen? Several tribe

It was a sad day for the Moqui tribe when Achew cought a evil fish with one fin in the Amazon River. Some people said, "Let's throw the fish in the River,"
The chif said, "no bring bad luck to river." Some said, Burn it witch Doctor said. Bring bad luck in air old witch Doctor Found a book They said, if you tuch eye balls evil spirits willcome,

members had suggestions; to each the chief responded in traditional laconic Indian phrases. One girl later caught the rhythm of his remarks in a story she wrote about the adventures of our tribe. So no one touched the eyeballs, and the tribe decided to risk burning the fish, but that was not the end of their troubles. Again to quote from a child's paper:

We started to get wood and we made A circle with stones around the fire So the fire wouldn't spread, and we waited and waited, and when the fire went out, the bones were still there.

Fear remained with the bones. The next day the white men came (actually two volunteers who agreed to leave their tribal roles temporarily). The tribe heard the worst. They were going to have to leave the valley they loved. To intensify that moment, I stood up, holding my baby in my arms, and said, "The ghosts of our fathers still fish this sacred river. I shall not live to see our children grow up apart from the power of this tribe." I pressed them, in role all the while, to sense the desperation of a people who could not contemplate going on without the symbol of their heritage, in this case a sacred river. Because by this time I was clearly one of their tribe and not a teacher, my attitude could not be considered alien. The problem I faced was their problem, too. They began to pick up the challenge my somber decision posed.

"Maybe we could let these babies live and just not have any more."

"Maybe we could move somewhere else."

I shook my head slowly. "But our children would never know this valley."

Again the tribe wanted to fight the white men. "It's not fair; we'll have to kill them, not our own babies."

As we talked, the river slowly began to rise. The children backed up reluctantly, gathering their baskets and spears as they watched the water inch toward their homes. One brave tribesman refused to move; instead he stood firm as the water rose around him. Soon he was swimming in defiance of the flood.

It was then that two tribe members, whom I had coached before the drama began, came up to the group in role as very reasonable, not hostile, not armed white men. (I had no intention of triggering their will to fight.) These men offered us another valley, just as good, but one that would not be flooded. The tribe members were visibly relieved. The prospect of killing our babies, whom most of the girls and I were by this time cradling in our arms, was too horrible to contemplate. Our right brains told us genocide was insane.

The next task was to get ready for the journey. In role I pressed the group again. We could not just pack up; we had to face the fact that the journey would be long and difficult; we could carry with us only what we could pack on our backs. One boy insisted we had horses, but I quickly jumped in to note that these two horses (I couldn't make it one since he had used the plural noun) would have to be saved to carry the old and the sick. I wanted to sustain the pressure to decide what to leave behind. Before long the children themselves came up with principles of selection.

"Let's take the baby's cradle."

"No, we can make a new cradle; all we'll need to take is our tools."

In role still, I decided to take one thing we could show our children and grandchildren to let them know what this river valley was like. The class picked up this lead. The challenge was to right-brained symbol-making. One object would have to embody the essence of a culture, though, of course, none of those children could have verbalized this concept at this stage.

The next drama session we traveled--through jungle, over desert, across a wide river in canoes, which were hastily constructed on the spot--until we finally reached the new valley. It was perfect, of course. Before long the men were dragging in bear, deer, and whales for our lunch. In the meantime, I was making preparations for our first Council Fire in the new valley. One of the men found a cave, and we decided to make it our sacred gathering place; after we built up a good base for our Council Fire there, the chief called the tribe in and asked the witch doctor to light the fire. Then each of us hung onto the cave wall the one thing we had brought with us to remind us and our children of our sacred valley. I brought the old feathered ceremonial robe of our first chief; then Little Kitten, one of the oldest women of the tribe, came up with a necklace that had belonged to her great-great-grandfather, the first chief. On it we discovered an amulet that had great power. Another tribe member brought a stone from the Sacred Amazon so the River God would bless this new valley. Then came the expected weapons of all sorts. Finally, there was a magic stone the chief had brought. We all looked closely at it; then we called the witch doctor. One child saw an inscription, but none of us could make it out. We passed this imaginary stone from hand to hand slowly and in perfect silence. The moment was intense. Right brains were at work. At last, the old witch doctor, father of our present one, "read" the words: "Peace, power, love." We all knew this was indeed the law of our tribe.

What had happened? Certainly I hadn't taught in any traditional sense; I could never have predicted the outcome of this final moment. I simply stayed in role as a tribe member and set my right brain to work along with theirs. Between the 45-minute class sessions my co-teacher--who also worked in role as a tribe member--and I met to figure out how best to set up the beginning of the next session and how we would take whatever responses we thought the class might give us and focus these. Our goal was to provide pressure for making tough decisions whenever we could. What evolved went far beyond anything we had planned. What happened to those children was more than they could verbalize. They moved from a tribe intent on war to a group affirmation of peace, power, and love.

When I went back to that classroom four months after we had been in that Amazon valley together, I discovered that the experience they had had still lived. I asked them to draw a picture of one thing they remembered from our experience as a tribe. The bad luck fish, the journey, the problem of the babies, the names tribe members had given themselves--all were recalled. That experience had been internalized.

Out of significant experience such as this is likely to come learning that transforms consciousness. It is the kind of learning that can make people whole. Any activity that evokes a struggle with a profound human question is one that can provide pressure for right-brained learning. As we join our students in a group-created drama, we recover the imagining, playful child within ourselves. At the same time we engage in an act that is ancient. All primitive rituals have at their heart the assumption of role--wearing a mask, acting out fears or dreams, weaving the self into a group fantasy. This is the root act of intuition: knowing by entering into. Like primitive tribesmen who don masks, children who participate in educational drama take on the powers of adults, entering into a consciousness that expands their own. They intuit and know. The process of synthesis knits the strands of partial information into a warm blanket of understanding.

Here is another illustration. As part of a drama on monastic life of the Middle Ages, Dorothy Heathcote led a group of ten-year-old children to write diaries. The discipline of silence, rising to go to prayers at the sound of a bell, the long hours at the copying table, the scant food, the pain of bare feet on cold stone--all became real to one boy, who wrote:

> I walk back towards my cell, my stomach empty, my knees stiff from kneeling. I enter my stone room. A shaft of light falls upon my unfinished manuscript. My eyes glance up at the holy cross. My legs need rest, so I sit on my stone seat. The table, wooden, a privilege to use. On it, my sheet of vellum; also a fine quill, a pot of black ink. I borrow other colors from my fellow brothers. As I begin to sketch my design, I wonder, is this the right life?[17]

This boy put together his experience in a monastary in a way that reverberated with significance. His right hemisphere synthesized and gave meaning to his actions.

Ironically enough, the analytical half of the brain in its effort to clarify and order experience often creates its own confusion. It has difficulty uncluttering and getting to the heart of the matter. Joseph W. Meeker reminds us that because so much of American education is skewed to analytical thinking, students are often overwhelmed. The problem is not confined to students either. Meeker notes that most university scholars today "are found to be overwhelmed by the abundance and complexity of their pursuits.... Facts are everywhere, but they fail to come together."[18]

An in-depth experience with drama can help students take the facts they know and synthesize them into a whole so they can make sense of their world. This is not to say that drama will cleanse experience of its bewildering variety or mystery. The information available to us at any given moment in a drama is like that available in real life. It is never neat or linear. It comes at us in a swirling kaleidoscope of images and sensory data. In this chaos, we need to discern structure and pattern, but always a structure subject to transformation in the next moment. Drama reflects the reality of human experience. Any particular situation at any specific moment is alive with possibilities. Human beings must learn to thrive on the dynamics of these possibilities and on the subtle changes possible in any relationship.

Reprinted with permission from The North American Review, copyright © 1975 by the University of Northern Iowa.

The goal of drama is not to tend a fenced-in garden of left-brained knowledge. Instead it is to lead an expedition into the wilderness of the right brain--a region where interrelationship is what matters; where everything grows together, living in terms of, taking account of, but not destroying another; where there is no distinction between weed and flower, useless and useful.

Academic orderliness, the notion that information can and should be presented in only an isolated, linear, left-brained way, and its acquisition by students evaluated in terms of measurable behavioral change, must be recognized for what it is--not a mirror of the real world but instead a useful fiction invented by humans. Neat factual information is not all there is; it is not knowing in all its fullness. Mere left-hemisphere cognition denies the richness of experience, buying a tortured orderliness at the expense of wholeness and subjective reality. Linear thinking takes the world apart and outlines it. Right-brained knowing takes it all in and makes of it a synthesis, a vision of the whole. This wholeness is not a fiction, however; it is the nature of reality. As proclaimed in a space-filler in The Last Whole Earth Catalog: "We cannot put it all together; it is all together."

To develop as a full human being, one must see that his outer and inner world stay all together. All that the human race knows now and has ever known and believed to be true must exist side-by-side in an unsettling tension and ambiguity. If a person rejects nothing, he or she can view the knowledge and myths of our age in light of those of the past and vice versa. In that way we can keep the forgotten language of image and dream alive and powerful even as it is set next to scientific facts. These facts must stand under the pressure of the old truths.

Dorothy Heathcote once dramatized this tension between the new and the old by having a student in a high school drama class assume the attitude of a modern-day scientist and in that role deliver a lecture on the ecology of forests to an assembled corpus of learned colleagues. As he spoke, in walked the Druids, dressed in white. They challenged his truth with theirs based on observation, experience, and belief.

In another drama in which a researcher was photographing the sun, Heathcote arranged for Prometheus to enter and assert that he was much more daring back when the world was new, telling his story of stealing fire from the very hearth of the gods. In the dramatic confrontation, students were pushed to weather the ambiguity, to carry the imcompatible side-by-side, to achieve a synthesis with their right brains. As Heathcote has reminded us, we have no choice but to live in both worlds--the scientific left brain and the mythical right brain.[20]

William Blake, good poet that he was, was aware of the contradictions and complexities revealed in dark, right-brained image-making. He showed us that experience is not simply the opposite of innocence, for example. He had the courage not to shun his right-brained knowing to conform to or communicate with his powerful peers in the Age of Reason. How much easier it should be for us to dare to affirm a right-brained world view in a century shattered by the amorality of hollow left-brained power and manipulation. The eighteenth-century defenders of Reason were far more self-righteous than ours. In fact, it is our scientists themselves who are leading us--using, ironically enough, the most left-brained of laboratory tests--to verify truths glimpsed by poets. What is more, leading science educators such as Mary Budd Rowe are recognizing the value of putting strategies for left- and right-brained knowing side by-side in the classroom.[21] She suggests drawing imaginary fruit or flowers to juxtapose with and compare to precise drawings based on observation. She recognizes the validity of both modes of knowing. True scientists value invention. Bob Samples points out the absurdity of not doing so: "Whenever human beings say something in an ecology of overextended rationality [what psychologists have labeled the 'cognitive' domain], they are greeted with 'what evidence do you have to back that up?' This attitude discourages taking risks.... Paradoxical as it seems, the rational mind prefers the rules it invents to the process of invention."[22]

Paul Bradwein is another prominent educator who encourages teachers to let students have "the right to go back and forth naturally between fantasy and reality. When they work in narrow confines, they readily resort to stereotypes and truisms instead of seeking evidence to demonstrate their hypotheses."[23]

William Blake wrote, "Without contraries there is no progression."[24] As we educate students to the bias of our culture--scientific, verifiable, objective truth--we need to also introduce them to the contrary view--the primitive, cyclical, holistic synthesis shot through with the wisdom of survival.[25] Educational drama provides one of the most powerful ways to do this.

Into our fact-soaked psyches dramatic invention comes

splashing with a right-brained paddle. It is headed for a truth where mere facts are not what matter, for the deep knowing that makes information come alive, and for experience that breeds energy.

The wilderness of our right brain beckons. One nine-year-old summed up the feelings of many of us. He and his classmates were journeying back into time on an imagined Halloween night, and they became frightened. Dorothy Heathcote, who was leading this scarey drama, asked with concern, "Should we go forward, do you think? I feel very responsible for all our safety."

"Yes," came the boy's strong voice, "We must go forward now to find out all there is to know. We owe it to ourselves."[26]

References

[1]See, for example, Robert F. Mager, Preparing Instructional Objectives (Palo Alto, Calif.: Fearon Publishers, 1962), p. 13.

[2]Mark Phillips, "Confluent Education, the Hidden Curriculum, and the Gifted Child," Phi Delta Kappan, November 1976, p. 238.

[3]Michael S. Gazzaniga, "The Split Brain in Man," in Altered States of Awareness, Readings from "Scientific American," with introductions by Timothy J. Teyler (San Francisco: W. H. Freeman, 1972), pp. 119-124. Other good summaries of brain research are: Marilyn Ferguson, The Brain Revolution--The Frontiers of Mind Research (New York: Taplinger, 1973); Erwin Lausch, Manipulation--Dangers and Benefits of Brain Research (New York: Viking, 1972); and Wilder Penfield, The Mystery of the Mind--A Critical Study of Consciousness and the Human Brain (Princeton, N.J.: Princeton University Press, 1975). Ferguson's book is the most comprehensive, providing a good introduction to the subject, but it is somewhat choppy to read; Lausch's is the best written, and Penfield's the most rhapsodic.

[4]Jean Houston, "The Mind of Margaret Mead: How She Democratizes Greatness," Quest '77, July/August 1977, p. 22.

[5]Robert Ornstein, "The Duality of the Mind: A Symposium in Print with Paul Bradwein and Robert Ornstein,"

Instructor, January 1977, p. 56. See also James Moffett and Betty Jane Wagner, Student-Centered Language Arts and Reading, K-13, 2 ed. (Boston: Houghton Mifflin, 1976), pp. 461-462. Although he doesn't call his method right-brained, W. Timothy Gallway's "Self 2" is the non-verbal one in his Inner Tennis--Playing the Game (New York: Random House, 1976). What Peter Elbow calls freewriting is also right-brained. See his Writing without Teachers (New York: Oxford University Press, 1973).

[6]Charles Weingartner, "Ready on the Right--A Review and Analysis of Bob Samples' The Metaphoric Mind," Media and Methods, February 1977, p. 21. See also Joseph E. Bogen, "Educational Aspects of Hemispheric Specialization," and Harry J. Jerison, "Evolution of the Brain," U. C. L. A. Educator, Spring 1975.

[7]See Jerome S. Bruner, On Knowing; Essays for the Left Hand. New York: Atheneum, 1965.

[8]Robert E. Ornstein, The Psychology of Consciousness (New York: Viking, 1972), p. 162. See also the collection of readings he edited: The Nature of Human Consciousness (San Francisco: W. H. Freeman, 1973).

[9]Robert Assagioli, Psychosynthesis (New York: Viking, 1971), p. 217.

[10]Bob Samples, "Mind Cycles and Learning," Phi Delta Kappan, May 1977, p. 689. See also his The Metaphoric Mind (Reading, Mass.: Addison-Wesley, 1976) and The Wholeschool Book: Teaching and Learning Late in the Twentieth Century (Reading, Mass.: Addison-Wesley, 1977).

[11]Robert E. Ornstein, The Psychology of Consciousness, p. 219.

[12]Ibid., p. 119.

[13]Nigel Calder, Chapter 5, "An Inward Spaceflight," The Mind of Man (New York: Viking, 1970), pp. 81-95. See also Joseph Chilton Pearce, The Crack in the Cosmic Egg (New York: Julian Press, 1971).

[14]Mager, op. cit.

[15]See, for example, Ann Shaw, The Development of a Taxonomy of Educational Objectives in Creative Dramatics

in the United States Based on Selective Writings in the Field, M.A. thesis, Columbia University, 1968. Available through University microfilms, Ann Arbor, Mich., 1969.

[16]R. Baird Shuman introduced this news article as a starting point for a demonstration drama at the 1976 National Council of Teacher's of English meeting in Chicago. The anecdote which follows originally appeared in my article, "The Use of Role," Language Arts 55 (March 1978), 323-327.

[17]Betty Jane Wagner, Dorothy Heathcote--Drama as a Learning Medium (Washington, D.C.: National Education Association, 1976), pp. 195-196.

[18]Joseph W. Meeker, "Ambidextrous Education, or How Universities Can Become Unskewed and Learn to Live with the Wilderness," The North American Review, summer 1975, p. 45.

[19]Ibid., p. 40.

[20]For more illustrative dramas of this type, see Wagner, Chapter 14, "The Left Hand of Knowing," in Dorothy Heathcote--Drama as a Learning Medium.

[21]See Rowe's contrasts of the behaviorist's view with the humanist's view in Teaching Science as Continuous Inquiry (New York: McGraw-Hill, 1973).

[22]Bob Samples, The Metaphorical Mind.

[23]Paul Bradwein, "The Duality of the Mind: A Symposium in Print with Paul Bradwein and Robert Ornstein," Instructor, January 1977, p. 56.

[24]From The Marriage of Heaven and Hell.

[25]See Jonas Salk, The Survival of the Wisest (New York: Harper and Row, 1973).

[26]Wagner, Dorothy Heathcote, p. 172.

THE PLACE OF DRAMA IN TODAY'S HIGH SCHOOLS

R. Baird Shuman

The Anglo-American Conference on the Teaching of English held at Dartmouth College in 1966 left little question about the centrality of drama in the English curriculum. From that time to this, drama in all its forms has received increased attention in books and professional journals aimed at English teachers, most of whom have worked seriously and strenuously toward making drama in one or more of its many manifestations a part of their teaching.

Why Drama?

The English umbrella is large, and crowded under it are numerous elements of what is broadly referred to as "the English curriculum." The literature/grammar/composition tripod, for years the mainstay of English programs in this country, has now given way to more broadly conceived programs. Influential in this shift have been such seminal works as Jerome Bruner's The Process of Education (Cambridge, Mass.: Harvard University Press, 1961) which noted that knowledge is expanding so rapidly that it is important for today's youth to master modes of learning rather than to master accumulations of facts, many of which may be obsolete by the time they finish school. Charles Silberman's Crisis in the Classroom (New York: Random House, 1970) aired the author's well-documented contention that today's highly structured, overly formal schools threaten the well-being of the whole institution of education, and--more important--of many of the students served by these schools. Sidney Simon, Merrill Harmin, Louis Raths, Leland Howe and Howard Kirschenbaum have stressed the need for school curricula to put more emphasis on and provide more opportunity for values clarification, and such books as Values and Teaching (Columbus, Ohio: Charles E. Merrill Books, 1966) and Values Clarification (New York: Hart Publishing Co., 1972) have shown teachers methods of achieving this.

Drama has been seen by many, particularly in the last decade, to be one of the best means of helping students to know themselves more fully, and it is probable that during the next decade teachers generally and English teachers in particular will be giving more attention to the uses of drama in the schools. The Socratic imperative, "Know thyself," has special meaning in an age when man's identity is often threatened, in an age when isolated psychopaths attempt, for example, to escape their isolation and draw attention to themselves by acts of violence against public figures. Peter Slade makes a compelling point in his statement suggesting that "one of the most important reasons for developing child drama in schools generally is not actually a therapeutic one but the even more constructive one of prevention."[1] Youngsters who act out their internalized emotions, either through assuming roles in pre-existing plays or through engaging in the sort of creative dramatic activity demonstrated in the early 1920s by Winifred Ward and more recently by Dorothy Heathcote in her superb film, "The Death of a President," come to grips with their emotions, see themselves more dispassionately and objectively and, in healthy group activity, cope with the causes, effects and consequences of violent, anti-social behavior. The participants in such activities learn lessons that last a lifetime.

Merging formal drama with improvisation, students at the North Carolina Advancement School some years ago read West Side Story and then, with appropriate musical accompaniment from the phonograph record, acted out in slow motion the knife fight from the play. The result was on one level a rather impressive ballet; but on another, perhaps more impressive and important, level, a roomful of students (many with long histories of discipline problems) were acting out an aggressive and violent event in such a way that they could analyze and evaluate it as a clinical object, an object which mirrored for many of them an actuality from their own lives.

Where Does Drama Belong?

Because most school people are forced to think in a proprietary way and because school budgets and personnel must be allocated to specific areas within schools, one must ask where drama belongs in the school. To answer the question, one must point out that drama involves an enormous number and variety of activities and can lead to a great diversity of outcomes. For example, drama can be taught as a literary genre like poetry or the novel or the short story, in which instance drama might be read and discussed much as any other work of literature is read and discussed. Drama can be approached from the standpoint of readers' theater or chamber theater, a process which involves having students within a classroom situation assume roles within plays which are read aloud. Another approach to drama is that of learning the art of mime or of role-playing or simulation. Yet another approach, and one which has gained considerable favor of late, is that of improvisational drama or creative dramatics. All of these varieties of approaching drama might be found in a typical English department, although other secondary school departments might use some of them as well.[2]

Drama performed for public audiences is also supported by many schools; and while supervisory personnel is often drawn from English departments, the money for staging such plays is usually drawn from the general fund of the school, generally with the expectation that ticket sales will restore such monies as have been advanced. This sort of dramatic activity is most frequently viewed as extra-curricular.

What Does Drama Do for People?

Drama has been variously defined. James Moffett writes: "Drama is any raw phenomena as they are first being converted to information by some observer."[3] Brian Way considers drama to be that which is "concerned with experience by the participants, irrespective of any function of communication to an audience."[4] William Butler Yeats calls drama "a moment of intense life... an activity of the souls of the characters."[5] Dorothy Heathcote contends that drama is "a real man in a mess."[6]

Regardless of definition, drama touches the lives of men and women poignantly and directly. Anton Chekhov attributed to drama lofty qualities when he wrote, "Flies purify the air, and plays--the morals."[7] Federico García Lorca went even further when he asserted: "A nation which does not help and does not encourage its theater is, if not dead, dying; just as the theater which does not feel the social pulse, the historical pulse, the drama of its people, and catch the genuine color of its landscape and of its spirit, with laughter or with tears, has no right to call itself a theater, but an amusement hall, or a place for doing that dreadful thing known as 'killing time'."[8]

In a prophetic statement pointing in the direction of Winifred Ward, Dorothy Heathcote and other yet unborn giants in the field of creative dramatics, Henrik Ibsen in 1874 wrote: "A student has essentially the same task as the poet: to make clear to himself, and thereby to others, the temporal and eternal questions which are astir in the age and in the community to which he belongs."[9] Drama in Ibsen's view--and in the view of many astute educators who have lived during the century since he publicly uttered this sentiment--is basic to man's understanding of who and what he is, how his society operates and how his fellow beings function.

Drama as a Literary Genre

The student of literature must be exposed to drama as a type of literature. His exposure often involves essentially the reading of plays, a skill which some students develop only with considerable difficulty. Drama is more complicated in many respects than are such other genres as the novel or the short story. It is often more complicated even than poetry. This is largely because "drama mixes the other arts with a fine disregard, calling at will upon ingredients which seem to belong to painting and sculpture, dance and music, poetry and the novel. We must be careful therefore not to think only of the last two in this astonishing list. Visual and aural, mimetic and verbal, all are facets of the one art of drama: reading the play, we dare not ignore this fact."[10] If students are simply set loose to read plays, they likely will experience difficulty in coping with the intricacies of stage directions and with being able to imagine the visual and aural experiences upon which most plays so heavily depend. The teacher must prepare students to meet this problem by reading with them at the beginning, while helping them to create in their minds' eyes and ears the visual and aural effects suggested in the directions.

The teacher must also be aware that, whereas the

writer of a novel, short story or poem is, through words, communicating directly with the reader, the playwright does not usually have a reader in mind when he is writing. Rather, he uses words which actors and directors in turn must interpret for an audience. This makes the reading of a play a more artificial activity than the reading of, let us say, a poem. Styan notes this difference in his statement: "Drama is a social activity; reading poetry is usually a private one."[11]

Because drama is essentially a social activity, it is probably well that teachers minimize, though not abandon completely, the silent reading of plays and attempt instead, if they are seeking to teach drama as a literary genre, to expose students to live productions of plays where this is possible and to television, motion picture and recorded versions of plays where live productions are not available.

Readers' Theater

Readers' theater--or chamber theater, as it is sometimes called--is a flexible form of dramatic art that can be very useful to teachers dealing with drama. From the standpoint of basic skills, this form of drama helps students to develop reading and listening skills and also has the potential to lead the student to making intelligent critical judgments about plays.

Readers' theater may be formal or informal, spontaneous or rehearsed. Essentially it consists of having the participants assume roles in a play and act out these roles while reading their parts aloud rather than reciting memorized lines. On a formal level, such readings may be rehearsed for presentation to audiences. They may be staged with elaborate props and intricate lighting and musical effects. But typically in the high school classroom students simply read parts from a play like Thornton Wilder's *Our Town* or Eugene O'Neill's *The Hairy Ape*, presenting the play without props and without memorizing the lines. If the aim is a somewhat polished reading, roles may be assigned in advance and students asked to rehearse them at home. More often, roles are assigned in class and the reading begins immediately. The best method of proceeding can be judged by the teacher who knows whether the students are fairly effective sight readers or not.

The value of oral reading has been tested in a number of research studies with conflicting conclusions. Significant among these is Paul Campbell's study indicating that in the case of poetry, at least, there was considerably greater retention of facts, as measured by a true-false test on content, in the silent reading condition.[12] However, Daniel Witt's study indicates that Readers' Theater presentations were considered more "valuable" and "serious" than the same literature read silently.[13]

Mime, Role Playing and Simulation

Students who attempt to act need to learn how to move, how to use their bodies as vehicles of communication. They must also learn how to assume roles, cast themselves in identities not their own. It is helpful for them to be involved in simulation which forces them into thought patterns ascribed to someone who may be drastically unlike them.

The starting point in such activities is simple miming: walk as though you had a stone in the heel of your right shoe; now walk as though the ground is wet and you have a hole in the sole of your shoe; now walk as though you have borrowed a pair of shoes much too big for you. Or mime an emotion: it is Christmas morning and you open a large, beautiful wrapped package, only to discover that it contains a well-worn pair of blue jeans; but your father asks, "What is that in the pocket?" and you reach in to find the very wristwatch that you have been looking at in the jewelry store window for the past six months. This sort of activity should move from individual miming to miming with one or two other students and ultimately to group miming.

Simulation necessitates role playing, although role playing may be done independently of simulation. One effective approach to role playing is that used by the so-called "method" actors who employed the "Stanislavsky method" of trying to find in their own past experience emotions to dwell upon similar to the emotions they were to portray in a given role.

Simulation games such as Tripoli are easily available for purchase and they span most subject areas found in secondary schools. Teachers can also make up simulation games such as the "You are safe in an underground shelter following a nuclear attack; 22 other people are in the shelter with you" one [See pp. 54-5]. The dialogue in both simulation games and role playing situations is improvisational.

Creative Dramatics

Creative or improvisational dramatics may involve some assigned role-playing initially. For example, while the dramatic situation may not yet have been decided upon in any specific way (such decisions being left to the students who will take part in and create the drama), the students may find that one of their fellows is sitting at a desk on which a sign reads, "Lillian Hunter, Senior Ward Nurse, Intensive Care Unit." Where such is the case, it is obvious that the drama is likely to be made around a hospital situation and would involve a critical health problem. If, on the other hand, the sign read, "Wilbur Hayes, Register of Wills," the ensuing situation would probably have to do with the question of inheritance.

Much creative dramatics does not involve this sort of direction. Very often the teacher begins by engaging the students in informal conversation, using this opportunity to build rapport and to make the students feel secure in the situation being created. The teacher must make the students feel certain that they will not be let down, that they will not be permitted to fail within the drama once the action has begun. I usually say, "I will not allow you to fail. I will rescue you if you need it--but I don't really think that I will have to rescue you." And seldom have I had to impose myself on the situation because a participant could not keep the dialogue going.

It is very important that students be impressed by the seriousness of making a play. The teacher must not skimp on preparation time, for if he does, the drama may degenerate into silliness before it is half done. I build the framework for preventing this by saying something like, "Once you assume your character, you cease, for the time, to be you. You become someone else, possibly someone quite different from your real self. If you do not, within the drama, become this other person, you may destroy the drama we are trying to make. It is perfectly normal that you may feel odd or embarrassed or selfconscious at some time along the way. If you do, please do not destroy the drama; rather, just step aside for the moment and stay out of the drama until you can reenter it and control yourself." This admonition has consistently worked for me, but more important, it has forced students to accept responsibility for their own behavior. At the secondary school level, there probably is no more important lesson for students to learn than that of accepting responsibility for the way they act.

The proper use of creative dramatics within the classroom has so many valuable outcomes that to list them would be to double the length of this chapter. Perhaps it is sufficient to say that students who are properly led into creative dramatics activities begin, with a high level of genuine excitement and enthusiasm, to learn basic skills because they have need to use these skills if they are to make their dramas convincing. Creative dramatics leads students into true life situations in which the problems to be coped with are real problems for which real solutions must be found. Within the classroom, without props, without costumes, drama--make-believe, if you will--becomes for a time reality, which, when properly done, it is, because the universals of the situation are realities even though the details may be fabricated.

Creative dramatics is an impressive vehicle for leading students into an understanding of their own deepest feelings and to their own intrinsic personality as it relates to society. It does this by moving students into areas of time and space apart from those they are most familiar with and allowing them to create intense and cogent situations within which they, having assumed--and, indeed, created--a persona, can use that persona as a mirror of their own most real selves. And despite the fact that the performance is seen by all the other participants, the individual privacy and integrity of each participant are protected.

Plays for an Audience

The final aspect of drama that will be treated in this chapter is that which produces a tangible, demonstrable outcome in the form of a well-rehearsed and somewhat polished production for an audience. The school play allows students of varying abilities to be involved creatively in a major extracurricular activity whose success is dependent upon its enlisting the talents of actors, musicians, dancers, directors and (in some cases) writers, as well as those of students competent in electricity, carpentry, painting, printing, sewing and a host of other skills. Probably the school drama provides an outlet for a more diverse group of students than any other school activity. The student who is weak academically can work side-by-side--and on an equal footing--with the student who is academically talented. The non-reader can be as fully involved as the speed reader. The shy, retiring artist can contribute significantly without ever being exposed to that direct contact with an audience which he might find threatening; yet, by making his contribution well, he might be moving several steps toward building the kind of self-confidence which will eventually make him less shy and retiring.

The school play is truly a school-wide activity and also serves the valuable function of bringing the school and the community closer together. In some states, state-wide drama contests add yet another dimension to plays done primarily for an audience. Such contests, which usually involve valuable critiquing sessions by competent drama critics, are extremely valuable to the students involved in them, largely because they enable students to bring a school activity into the real world, into a realistically competitive arena where the work is taken very seriously by professionals who believe firmly in the importance of drama.

Parting Thoughts

Art has been said to imitate reality. Probably no form of art captures the essence of reality more nearly than drama in all its aspects. Acting, writing, stagecraft, reading, moving, singing, speaking, dancing, critiquing: these are all major parts of dramatic activity. Drama is discovery in the best sense, but it is also invention. It is complicated and sophisticated even in its simplest forms, yet it is accessible to people of all persuasions and abilities. If our schools would heed the current cry to return to the basics, probably drama is the area to which they might most legitimately return, for within drama are to be found the most enduring fundaments of human society and endeavor.

References

[1] Child Drama (New York: Philosophical Library, 1955), p. 119.

[2] For example, one might read about the uses to which drama might be put in other disciplines by referring to some of the following: C. Paxton, "Play as an Effective

Aid for Teaching FLES," Hispania 45 (December 1962), 756-758; Sister Margeretta, "Foreign Language Dramatizations," Catholic School Journal 64 (February 1964), 64-65; B. M. McIntyre, "Creative Dramatics in the Reading Program," Pittsburgh University Conference on Reading (1955), pp. 143-45; Sister Mary Demetria, "We Wrote a Vocational Play," Catholic School Journal 64 (March 1964), 53; M. D. Headley, "Science and Scenarios," School and Community 50 (November 1963), 19; M. S. Woods, "Creative Dramatics: An Exciting Way to Teach Safety," Safety Education 43 (May 1964), 14-17; W. M. Zinmaster, "Contributions of Creative Dramatics to Teaching Social Studies," Speech Teacher 14 (November 1965), 305-313.

[3]Drama: What Is Happening (Urbana, Ill.: NCTE, 1967), p. 1.

[4]Development through Drama (London: Longmans, Green, 1966), p. 3.

[5]Plays and Controversies (London: Macmillan, 1923), pp. 91-92.

[6]In her film, "Three Looms Waiting."

[7]Letters on the Short Story, the Drama and Other Literary Topics, Louis S. Friedland, ed. (New York: Minton, Balch, 1924), p. 170.

[8]"The Prophecy of Lorca," Theatre Arts, October 1950, p. 38.

[9]"Speech to the Norwegian Students, September 10, 1874," Speeches and New Letters, Arne Kildal, trans. (Boston: Richard G. Badger, 1910), pp. 50-51.

[10]J. L. Styan, The Dramatic Experience (Cambridge, England: Cambridge University Press, 1965), p. 5.

[11]Styan, p. 2.

[12]"An Experimental Study of the Retention and Comprehension of Poetry Resulting from Silent Reading and from Oral Interpretation," doctoral dissertation, University of Southern California, 1960.

[13]"A Comparative Analysis of Audience Response to

Realistic and Anti-Realistic Drama Where Perceived through Acting, Readers Theatre, and Silent Reading," doctoral dissertation, University of Denver, 1962.

ANNOTATED BIBLIOGRAPHY

R. Baird Shuman

Atkinson, Claudene D. "A New Approach: Drama in the Classroom," English Journal 60 (October 1971), 947-56. An important article, aimed at highschool English teachers who wish to use dramatics as a significant educational medium.

Ayllon, Maurie, and Susan Snyder. "Behavioral Objectives in Creative Dramatics," Journal of Educational Research 62 (April 1969), 355-359. Discusses creative dramatics in terms of measurable outcomes.

Barnes, Douglas, ed. Drama in the English Classroom, Urbana, Ill.: National Council of Teachers of English, 1968. An outgrowth of the Dartmouth Conference of 1966, this book presents the British view of how drama can be used effectively in classroom settings.

Barnfield, Gabriel. Creative Drama in the Schools, New York: Hart Pub. Co., 1968. Focuses attention on improvisation and its possibilities as an educational tactic. A much-needed book in its time, its suggestions and comments are still relevant.

Bertram, Jean. "Creative Dramatics in the School," Elementary English 35 (December 1958), 515-518. An early article which focuses on the elementary school, but has suggestions which teachers at other levels might employ in their teaching.

Birdwhistell, Ray L. Kinesics and Context: Essays on Body Motion Communication, Philadelphia: University of Pennsylvania Press, 1970. A fundamental book for one who would proceed very deeply into the area of educational drama. Excellent documentation, exciting conclusions.

Blackmur, R. P. Language as Gesture: Essays in Poetry, New York: Harcourt, Brace & World, 1952. The title essay is relevant to educational drama inasmuch as it deals in a concentrated way with elements of communication relating to language and kinesics.

Boocock, Sarane S., and James S. Coleman. "Games with Simulated Environments in Learning," Sociology of Education 39 (summer 1966), 215-236. A central article for teachers outside English who wish to involve students in simulations, role playing, and dramatic activities related to the learning process and the substance of the discipline.

Borton, Terry. Reach, Touch, and Teach, New York: McGraw-Hill, 1970. An affective approach to learning; much concerned with kinesics and proxemics.

Brack, Kenneth. "Creative Dramatics: Why? How? When?" Elementary English 36 (December 1959), 565-567. Valuable in that it suggests when this technique should not be used as when it should.

Brewbaker, James M. "Simulation Games and the English Teacher," English Journal 61 (January 1972), 104-109. A good adjunct to the Boocock-Colemen article.

Brown, George I. Human Teaching for Human Learning: An Introduction to Confluent Education, New York: Viking, 1971. The concern in this book is largely with student involvement in the learning process at all levels. Deals with the humanizing potential of education; stresses creativity.

Calabria, Frances R. "The Why of Creative Dramatics," Instructor 77 (August 1967), 182. A brief rationale for using dramatic techniques in the classroom; persuasive.

Carlson, Bernice Wells, and David R. Gingeland. Play Activities for the Retarded Child, New York: Abingdon Press, 1961. An early, insightful study, particularly interesting in the light of Heathcote's films Three Looms Waiting (1971) and Who's Handicapped (1973).

Chambers, Dewey W. Storytelling and Creative Drama, Dubuque, Iowa: Wm. C. Brown, 1970. Primarily for elementary school teachers. Employs many of the techniques pioneered by Winifred Ward; a fine resource.

Christensen, J. A. "School Drama," Media & Methods 8 (January 1972), 33. A very brief overview.

Coggin, Philip A. The Uses of Drama, New York: George Braziller, 1956. An omnibus approach to the uses of drama in society. Good background reading.

Corsini, Raymond. Role Playing in Psychotherapy, Chicago: Aldine, 1966. While the book is somewhat specialized, the techniques suggested for role playing are excellent and would be easily adaptable to classroom drama situations.

Cottrell, June. Teaching with Creative Dramatics, Skokie, Ill.: National Textbook, 1975. Focus is on young students; suggests many stories appropriate for use with students. Emphasizes the need to allow spontaneous play of the child to be a basis for dramatic activity.

Crosby, Muriel. "Creative Dramatics as a Developmental Process," Elementary English 33 (January 1956), 13-18. A sagacious article, carefully reasoned and appealingly presented.

Crystal, Josie. "Role-Playing in a Troubled Class," Elementary School Journal 69 (January 1969), 169-179. A happy marriage of psychology and drama. Intelligent and practical approach to classroom control through dramatic involvement of students.

Daigon, Arthur, and Ronald LaConte. Challenge and Change in the Teaching of English, Boston: Allyn & Bacon, 1971. Dorothy Heathcote's chapter, "Drama," is forceful and clear.

DeMille, Richard. Put Your Mother on the Ceiling: Children's Imagination Games, New York: Viking, 1973. Ideas of how to use games to stimulate the imagination of young students.

Dennison, George. The Lives of Children, New York: Random House, 1969. While Dennison does not specifically deal with educational drama, his compassionate assessment of the school situation is valuable background reading for any teacher who would employ the technique.

Dixon, John. "Creative Expression in Great Britain," English Journal 57 (September 1968), 795-802. Concerning itself largely with providing a rationale for drama in the schools, the article is a result of Dixon's involvement in the Dartmouth Conference.

Dodd, Nigel, and Winifred Hickson, eds. Drama and Theatre in Education, London: Heinemann, 1973. Of special value are Gavin Bolton's chapter on current attitudes toward drama in the schools, John Hodgson's chapter on improvisation, and Dorothy Heathcote's chapter on the needs of the drama teacher.

Downs, Genevieve R., and Allan M. Pitkanen. "Therapeutic Dramatics for Delinquent Boys," Clearing House 27 (March 1953), 423-426. Especially valuable when read in connection with Josie Crystal's article and in the light of Heathcote's film, Improvised Drama, Part I (1966) which deals with the making of a drama by a group of boys in a Scottish facility for delinquents.

Duke, Charles R. "Creative Dramatics: A Natural for the Multiple Elective Program," Virginia English Bulletin 21 (winter 1971), 9. A brief article which shows how creative dramatics can be used as a nine- or 12-week elective course in English departments at the secondary level.

_______. Creative Dramatics and English Teaching, Urbana, Ill.: National Council of Teachers of English, 1974. Presents an historical and philosophical background for creative dramatics. More than half the book is devoted to practical teaching methodologies. The handbook of resources is particularly valuable.

Dumas, Wayne. "Role Playing: Effective Technique in the Teaching of History," Clearing House 44 (April 1970), 468-470. Makes suggestions applicable to all the social studies.

Durland, Frances Caldwell. Creative Dramatics for Children, Yellow Springs, Ohio: Antioch Press, 1952. A strong book in its day; has since been superseded by a number of more current works.

Ebbitt, Paul F. "Drama for Slow Learners," English Journal 52 (November 1963), 624-626. Still a valuable resource for teachers who work with students having short attention spans and learning disabilities.

Ehrlich, Harriet W., ed. Creative Dramatics Handbook, Urbana, Ill.: National Council of Teachers of English, 1974. Originally written for the Philadelphia Board of Education, the book shows how creative dramatics can improve students' language skills. Hundreds of practical suggestions, particularly for the elementary school classroom.

Elkind, Samuel. Improvisation Handbook, Glenview, Ill.: Scott, Foresman, 1976. A teacher resource which suggests games that might lead to creative dramatic activities; presents scenes for performance by students.

Fast, Julian. Body Language, New York: Pocket Books, 1971. Goes into kinesics very well. A useful adjunct to Hall's The Silent Language.

Fines, John, and Raymond Verrier. The Drama of History: An Experiment in Co-operative Teaching, London: New University Education, 1974. The book tells of how the writers experimented in a cooperative teaching project using methods they had learned from Dorothy Heathcote.

Frazier, Clifford. Discovery in Drama, New York: Paulist Press, 1969. Some keen insights into the affective nature of drama.

Gerbrandt, Gary L. An Idea Book for Acting Out and Writing Language, K-8, Urbana, Ill.: National Council of Teachers of English, 1974. More than 700 activities are suggested for implementing dramatic activity in the elementary school. Many ideas easily adaptable for use at other academic levels.

Graubard, Paul S. "Pantomime: Another Language," Elementary English 37 (May 1960), 302-306. Useful suggestions for means of introducing students to pantomiming, proceeding logically from the short and simple to the longer, more complex uses of this technique.

Gross, Ronald, and Beatrice Gross. Radical School Reform, New York: Simon & Schuster, 1969. See especially Farnum Gray's contribution on the Pennsylvania Advancement School in which dramatic activities were used significantly, as they were also in the North Carolina Advancement School in Winston-Salem.

Hall, Edward T. The Hidden Dimension, Garden City, N.Y.: Doubleday, 1969. A necessary reading experience for any teacher who would use dramatic techniques in teaching, since Hall deals with the uses of space (proxemics) and with many phases of human communication.

________. The Silent Language, Greenwich, Conn.: Fawcett Publications, 1959. Deeply concerned with gesture, movement, physical reaction. A must for teachers who have a desire to use creative dramatics as a teaching device. A brilliant perspective on communication.

Harris, Peter, ed. Drama in Education, London: Bodley Head, 1967. A timely book, coming soon after the Dartmouth Conference and giving an accurate status statement on drama as the British used it in schools at that time. See especially Heathcote's chapter, "Improvisation."

Heathcote, Dorothy. "How Does Drama Serve Thinking, Talking, and Writing?" Elementary English 47 (December 1970), 1077-1081. Places drama into the natural and normal context of the classroom and relates it to the teaching of skills.

Hirsch, Werner Z., ed. Inventing Education for the Future, San Francisco: Chandler, 1967. A number of the chapters in this valuable book focus on the use of drama as an effective teaching device.

Hodgson, John, and Martin Banham, eds. Drama in Education: The Annual Survey, New York: Pitman, 1972. An annual publication which surveys the year of drama in education. Extremely valuable in the first of these surveys (1972) is Dorothy Heathcote's "Training Needs for the Future."

________, and E. Richards. Improvisation, London: Methuen, 1966. One of the most complete books on the subject.

Hoetker, James. Dramatics and the Teaching of Literature, Urbana, Ill.: National Council of Teachers of English, 1969. An especially valuable resource for secondary school teachers who wish to involve students in the active experiencing of literature.

________. Students as Audiences, Urbana, Ill.: National

Council of Teachers of English, 1971. Gives research evidence of the relationship between the study of drama in the classroom and students' attendance of theatrical productions.

Holbrook, David, ed. English for the Rejected Child, London: Cambridge University Press, 1964. Particularly cogent is Geoffrey Hawkes' chapter, "Dramatic Work for the Backward Child."

Johnson, Kenneth R. "Black Kinesics: Some Non-Verbal Communication Patterns in Black Culture," Florida FL Reporter 9 (spring-fall 1971), 17. Succinct and direct; invaluable for teachers of black youngsters as well as for those who would teach by dramatic techniques.

Jones, Catherine J. "The Creativity Problem," Illinois Schools Journal 51 (spring 1971), 2-9. A detailed article on the anatomy of creativity; keen and insightful.

Jones, Richard M., ed. Contemporary Educational Psychology: Selected Essays, New York: Harper & Row, 1967. The teacher interested in creative dramatics will profit from reading Aldous Huxley's contribution, "Education on the Non-Verbal Level."

Judy, Stephen, ed. Lecture Alternatives in Teaching English, Urbana, Ill.: National Council of Teachers of English, 1971. See particularly Mary Clare Yates' "Choose Your Environment," pp. 48-56.

Keyes, George. "Creative Dramatics and the Slow Learner," English Journal 54 (February 1965), 81-84. Particularly valuable when read in combination with Ebbitt's article and Holbrook's book.

Koziol, Stephen M., Jr. "Dramatization and Educational Objectives," English Journal 62 (November 1973), 1167-1170. Makes the differentiation between drama as "an object of study and a dynamic of action." Focuses on the process of drama.

Laban, Rudolf. The Mastery of Movement, Boston: Plays, Inc., 1971. Read in combination with Hall's The Silent Language and Fast's Body Language.

McCalib, Paul T. "Intensifying the Literary Experience

through Role-playing," English Journal 57 (January 1968), 41-46. Broader than the Magers article; interesting in combination with it.

McCaslin, Nellie. Creative Dramatics in the Classroom, New York: David McKay, 1968. A landmark book; aimed at the elementary school classroom.

McIntyre, Barbara M. "Creative Dramatics," Education 79 (April 1959), 495-498. Gives particular attention to the skills of articulation that students gain through creative dramatics.

________. "The Effect of Creative Activities on the Articulation Skills of Children," Speech Monograph (1958), pp. 42-48. A convincing rationale for engaging students in creative dramatics to make them more expressive.

Magers, Joan. "Role-playing Technique in Teaching a Novel," English Journal 57 (October 1968), 990-991. An interesting and practical method of involving students in literary study through dramatic activities.

Mead, Margaret, and Martha Wolfenstein, eds. Childhood in Contemporary Cultures, Chicago: University of Chicago Press, 1955. A book that teachers need to read. While it does not discuss educational drama in any concentrated way, it has broad implications for teachers who would use this medium with students.

Michael, William R., ed. Teaching for Creative Endeavor, Bloomington: Indiana University Press, 1968. Considers the whole gamut of creative activities available to teachers, giving intelligent emphasis to drama.

Moffett, James. Drama: What Is Happening?, Urbana, Ill.: National Council of Teachers of English, 1967. Another spin-off from the Dartmouth Conference. Demonstrates how drama can be used in informal educational settings.

________, and B. J. Wagner. Student-Centered Language Arts and Reading, K-13. Boston: Houghton Mifflin, 1976. Stresses involvement and informal learning. Includes much more emphasis on educational drama than the 1973 edition, by Moffett alone.

Mooney, Ross, and Taher A. Razik, eds. Explorations in

Creativity, New York: Harper & Row, 1967. Presents a coherent theory of creativity; includes chapters by most of the leaders in the field.

Muller, Herbert J. The Uses of English, New York: Holt, Rinehart & Winston, 1967. One of the two authorized reports of the Dartmouth Conference. Gives great attention to the use of drama in British schools.

Munch, Theo W. "A Sociodramatic Slant to Science Teaching," Science Education 37 (December 1953), 318-320. Suggests motivational devices that work as well today as they did when the article was written.

Pitcole, Marcia. "Black Boy and Role Playing: A Scenario for Reading Success," English Journal 57 (November 1968), 1140-1142. A specific methodology for involving poor readers in effective reading experiences through role playing.

Popovitch, James E. "Considerations in the Teaching of Creative Dramatics," Speech Teacher 8 (November 1959), 283-287. Gives a fine overview of what has been done in the field. A great deal is packed into a small space.

Rasmussen, Margaret, ed. Creative Dramatics, Washington, D.C.: Association for Childhood Education International, 1961. A stellar volume containing chapters by most of the leading lights in the field at that time. A Pre-Heathcote book, presenting the Winifred Ward approach quite fully.

Rogers, Carl. Freedom to Learn, Columbus, Ohio: Charles E. Merrill, 1969. A noted psychiatrist writes on how interpersonal relationships affect education. Especially valuable for its presentation of how "teacher-talk" affects the classroom environment

Ruesch, Jurgen, and Weldon Kees. Nonverbal Communication: Notes on the Visual Perception of Human Relations, Berkeley: University of California Press, 1956. A brilliant book; for the specialist rather than the neophyte.

Sayre, Gwenda. Creative Miming, London: Herbert Jenkins, 1959. The methods suggested here are a step toward improvisation and creative dramatics. The suggestions are practical.

Schools, Leo J. "Lifeboat," Media & Methods 7 (September 1971), 86. The technique suggested here has been much used in schools along with the "Fall-out Shelter" improvisation, which is an outgrowth of "Lifeboat."

Schwartz, Sheila. "Involving Students in the Drama Process, K-12," English Journal 63 (May 1975), 32-38. A very well documented article which concentrates on the process of drama in the classroom and suggests step-by-step techniques for its use.

________. "New Methods in Creative Dramatics," Elementary English 36 (November 1959), 484-487. An incisive, brief account of the rise in interest in the field at the elementary school level, detailing some techniques in use.

Shaftel, Fannie R. Role Playing for Social Values, Englewood Cliffs, N.J.: Prentice-Hall, 1967. One of the more important books for teachers. Particularly appropriate today in the light of the interest in values clarification and moral education.

________, and George Shaftel. Words and Actions: Role-Playing Photo-Problems for Young Children, New York: Holt, Rinehart & Winston, 1967. While the focus is on young children, the method is easily adaptable to older youngsters.

Sharpham, John R. "Some Approaches to Creative Drama at the Secondary Level in England," The Speech Teacher 24 (January 1975), 29-36. Discusses the role of the teacher and various instructional approaches.

Shelhammer, Lois B. "Solving Personal Problems through Sociodrama," English Journal 38 (November 1949), 503-505. An early article suggesting the use of drama as essentially a guidance device.

Shuman, R. Baird, ed. Creative Approaches to the Teaching of English: Secondary, Itasca, Ill.: F. E. Peacock, 1974. The longest chapter in the book (pages 39-100) is Charles Duke's chapter on drama. A portion of the chapter is devoted to educational drama.

________. "Drama in the Schools: A Well-Spring of Creativity," Journal of English Teaching Techniques 5 (Winter

1972), 16-22. Suggests means of encouraging student participation through drama.

________, ed. Questions English Teachers Ask, Rochelle Park, N.J.: Hayden Book Co., 1977. Contains a full section on drama in the schools, including creative dramatics.

Side, Ronald. "Creative Drama," Elementary English 46 (April 1969), 431-435. Something of an update of the Schwartz article of 1959.

Siks, Geraldine Brain. Children's Literature for Dramatization, New York: Harper & Row, 1964. A standard resource for elementary school students. Reminiscent of some of Winifred Ward's early books.

________. Drama with Children, New York: Harper & Row, 1977. Emphasizes activities that can be used with elementary school students.

________, and Hazel Dunnington, eds. Children's Theatre and Creative Dramatics, Seattle: University of Washington Press, 1961. One of the most complete and extensive books in its field. Despite its age, it is still an indispensable resource.

Silberman, Charles E. Crisis in the Classroom, New York: Random House, 1970. The book laments the formality and rigidity of schools and calls for more informality and flexibility. While the author does not go into detail about creative dramatics, he calls for the climate it can create.

Simon, Marianne P., and Sidney B. Simon. "Dramatic Improvisation: Path to Discovery," English Journal 54 (April 1965), 323-327. Shows means of employing creative dramatics as a means of self-discovery through values clarification.

Spolin, Viola. Improvisation for the Theater, Evanston, Ill.: Northwestern University Press, 1963. One of the most valuable overall books that any teacher can have; realistic and highly practical.

Summerfield, Geoffrey, ed. Creativity in English, Urbana, Ill.: National Council of Teachers of English, 1968. Of particular interest is David Holbrook's chapter, "Creativity in the English Programme."

Taylor, Loren E. Pantomime and Pantomime Games, Minneapolis: Burgess, 1965. A standard work in the field. Detailed explanations and suggestions of how to use pantomime to good effect.

Tiedt, Iris M., ed. Drama in Your Classroom, Urbana, Ill.: National Council of Teachers of English, 1974. Relate creative dramatics to regular classroom instruction. Suggestions for dramatization of stories, pantomime, puppetry.

Torrance, E. Paul. Encouraging Creativity in the Classroom, Dubuque, Iowa: Wm. G. Brown, 1970. Perhaps Torrance's most useful book for classroom teachers interested in how to identify and foster creativity in students.

Wagner, Betty Jane. Dorothy Heathcote: Drama as a Learning Medium, Washington, D.C.: National Education Association, 1976. More than just a biographical treatment, this book provides a realistic means of introducing teachers to the processes involved in educational drama.

________. "Evoking Gut-Level Drama," Learning 2 (March 1974), 16-20. Good insights into Heathcote's essential methodology. Practical, concise, incisive.

________. "The Use of Role," Language Arts 55 (March 1978), 323-327.

Walker, Kathrine Sorley. Eyes on Mime, New York: John Day, 1969. Not quite so useful to teachers as Taylor's book, but practical and imaginative nevertheless.

Ward, Winifred. "Creative Dramatics in the Elementary School," Quarterly Journal of Speech 28 (December 1942), 445-449. An important statement and explanation of what creative dramatics is and what it seeks to accomplish with young children.

________. Playmaking with Children, New York: D. Appleton-Century, 1957. Still a valuable resource for elementary school teachers.

Way, Brian. Development through Drama, London: Longman Group, 1967. Good insights, following the Dartmouth Conference, into the use the British have made of dramatic activities in the teaching situation.

Wilder, Rosilyn. A Space Where Anything Can Happen: Creative Drama in a Middle School, Rowayton, Conn.: New Plays Books, 1977. A valuable book both because it focuses on an age level that some teachers find difficult and because of its enthusiasm and conviction.

Wolfe, Jr., Denny T. "Creative Dramatics as a Tool for Teaching," North Carolina Education 6 (November 1975), 13-15. The author lists 16 skills that were taught in one creative dramatics encounter.

________, et al., eds. Action Learning: English/Language Arts, K-12, Raleigh, N.C.: North Carolina Department of Public Instruction, 1977. A practical and useful collection of lessons appropriate for classroom use. "Part III: Curriculum Drama," contains 10 practical strategies for the classroom as well as an overview essay and a bibliography.

Zuckerman, David W., and Robert E. Horn. The Guide to Simulation Games for Education and Training, Cambridge, Mass.: Information Resources, 1970. A valuable reference work which can be used effectively as an "ideabook."

NOTES ON THE CONTRIBUTORS

CHARLES R. DUKE is Professor of English at Plymouth State College of the University of New Hampshire, where he is involved in teacher training. He is author of Creative Dramatics and English Teaching, published by the National Council of Teachers of English in 1974. He contributed the chapter on drama to Creative Approaches to the Teaching of English: Secondary, published by the F. E. Peacock Publishing Company in 1974. The author of scores of articles, Professor Duke was a presenter at the 1976 Pre-Convention Workshop in Educational Drama which the National Council of Teachers of English sponsored. He was a contributor to Questions English Teachers Ask, published by the Hayden Book Company in 1977.

JAN A. GUFFIN is associate chairperson of the Department of English at North Central High School in Indianapolis, Indiana, and has been a member of the associate faculty at Indiana University-Purdue University. Mr. Guffin's doctoral dissertation was "Winifred Ward: A Critical Biography" (Duke University, 1975). He has served as a consultant to the Educational Testing Service and is a reader in English for the Advanced Placement Examinations. He has served as coordinator of language arts at the Duke University Demonstration School in Durham, North Carolina. He contributed the chapter on writing to Creative Approaches to the Teaching of English: Secondary and is the author of numerous articles. Mr. Guffin was a contributor to Questions English Teachers Ask. He was a presenter at the 1976 Pre-Convention Workshop in Educational Drama which the National Council of Teachers of English sponsored.

DOROTHY HEATHCOTE is perhaps the most renowned practitioner of educational drama in the world today. Senior lecturer in educational drama at the University of Newcastle-upon-Tyne in England, Ms. Heathcote has worked with teachers and students throughout the world. Her films, the most notable of which are Dorothy Heathcote Talks to Teachers, Improvised Drama I and Improvised Drama II, and Three Looms Waiting, have been seen by millions of educators. Ms. Heathcote's work has been published in Elementary English and in numerous anthologies. She is a frequent workshop leader in the United States and has done extensive in-service work with teachers at Northwestern and at Wake Forest universities.

R. BAIRD SHUMAN is Professor of English and Director of English Education at the University of Illinois at Urbana-Champaign. The author of three critical biographies of modern dramatists, Mr. Shuman directed the 1976 Pre-Convention Workshop in Educational Drama sponsored by the National Council of Teachers of English. Mr. Shuman edited Creative Approaches to the Teaching of English: Secondary (1974) and Questions English Teachers Ask (1977). He is the author of a broad range of articles which have appeared in such publications as PMLA, Modern Philology, American Literature, South Atlantic Quarterly, English Journal, Elementary English, English Education, and Education Digest.

BETTY JANE WAGNER is chair of the Department of English at the National College of Education in Evanston, Illinois. Mrs. Wagner is author of the first book to describe and explain Dorothy Heathcote's mode of using drama in the classroom. Her book, Dorothy Heathcote: Drama as a Learning Medium, was published in 1976 by the National Education Association. She is coauthor with James Moffett of Student-Centered Language Arts and Reading, K-13, published in 1976 by the Houghton Mifflin Company. She is a consultant and writer for Learning Magazine, having coauthored both A Learning Handbook, and Making and Using Inexpensive Classroom Media. She was a major author of Interaction: A Student-Centered Language Arts and Reading Program, a curriculum developed for Kindergarten through the first year of college under the senior editorship of James Moffett. It was published by Houghton Mifflin in 1973. At the National College of Education, Mrs. Wagner regularly teaches literature for children, theory and methods of teaching language arts, selection of school library materials, storytelling, the history of children's literature, Victorian prose and poetry, and composition in both the undergraduate and graduate schools. In addition, she regularly does demonstration lessons in the College's Demonstration School.

DENNY T. WOLFE, JR. is director of the Division of Languages of the North Carolina Department of Public Instruction and has been instrumental in promoting the cause of educational drama within the schools of his state. Mr. Wolfe's articles have appeared in such journals as Contemporary Education, The Clearing House, Reading Research Quarterly, and Exercise Exchange. He is coeditor of Action Learning and Writing in the Wild Young Spring published by the North Carolina Department of Public Instruction in 1977 and 1978 respectively. A presenter at the 1976 Pre-Convention Workshop in Educational Drama sponsored by the National Council of Teachers of English, Mr. Wolfe is also a member of the Nominating Committee of the Conference on English Education. He contributed to Questions English Teachers Ask. Mr. Wolfe has been an English department chairman at the secondary school level and has also taught English at the college level.

INDEX